# Child develc

CW00377307

About the author

Dr Vera Fahlberg, a psychotherapist with a paediatric background, is Medical Director of Forest Heights Lodge, Colorado, USA, a psychiatric treatment centre for emotionally-disturbed boys. She is consultant to various Departments of Social Services and is often called on to provide expert testimony in court cases involving children.

First published by
Michigan Department of Social Services 1982


Published by
British Agencies for Adoption & Fostering
11 Southwark Street
London SE1 1RQ

May 1982
reprinted August 1986

ISBN 0 903534 40 1
ISSN 0260-0803

# Acknowledgment

*BAAF* is grateful to Dr Vera Fahlberg for permission to publish three workbooks which she and her colleagues developed from the *Training of children in foster care* project co-sponsored by the Michigan Department of Social Services, Spaulding for Children of Michigan and Forest Heights Lodge, Evergreen, Colorado, with a grant from the Ed McConnell Foundation.

The workbooks, *Attachment and separation* (published by *BAAF* in October 1981), *Helping children when they must move* (published by *BAAF* in November 1981) and *Child development* were formulated, refined, and validated over a period of three years by 33 agencies involved in the training project.

Dr Fahlberg readily gave us permission to make minor changes to the text to make it applicable to the British scene. This has involved changes in spelling and some descriptions of procedures and facilities. In no way, however, has the core of the work been changed.

In the final section of this workbook we have substituted titles of some booklets published in this country for the American material, which might not be available here.

# Contents

# About this workbook

As children develop normally, they pass through a number of stages of development. At each of these stages, the child has to accomplish certain major developmental tasks. With each stage of development the child tends to exhibit certain physical, psychological, and emotional characteristics.

Although all children must accomplish the same developmental tasks, each individual child approaches them in a way that reflects his unique predispositions and experiences. The child's personality, physical abilities, and other individual attributes will certainly affect the way in which he exhibits the characteristics associated with a particular developmental stage. Nevertheless, there are significant common factors.

Ideally, families function to enable children to accomplish their developmental tasks. Within the family the child learns to value himself and to trust others. He learns about his own feelings and other people's. Within the family the child learns how to talk and how to think.

Families provide safety and security, stimulation and encouragement, and reasonable expectations and limits. Children need support and reasonable external controls as they meet each developmental challenge and cope with inevitable frustration in this process. Children who do not receive support become bewildered, insecure, and without self-esteem.

Knowledge of the tasks and characteristics associated with each stage of development is a key to helping a child. Parents who understand developmental issues are less likely to be as upset by normal behaviour and more likely to support the child as he struggles with the basic tasks at each stage. They are more readily able to perceive what a child needs to help him grow. They are more likely to meet his needs and his undesirable, but normal, behaviour will be unlikely to persist into later stages of development.

The perceptions, abilities, and behaviour of all children change as they mature. At each stage of development, children face challenges and difficulties. As they strive to meet these challenges, almost all children exhibit some behaviour that is not seen as particularly desirable by the families with whom they live. The fact that undesirable behaviour reflects normal development does not mean that it can be ignored; on the other hand, it does not need to be treated as an incurable disease or as reason to move a child from a family. Workers must be able to help families help children meet the challenges of normal development.

In addition, many children in placement have lived or are living i environments that are not conducive to achievement of the developmental tasks and thus their behaviour may reflect unmet developmental needs.

Since the physical, emotional, and psychological aspects of a chil development are so entwined, delays in one often affect subsequent development in other areas as well. The earlier environmental deprivation occurs, the more severe will be the effects. Many childre care must struggle if they are to overcome these complex and long lasting developmental delays.

It is important that social workers be able to distinguish between normal behaviour for varying ages and those patterns of behaviour th indicate unmet developmental needs. Knowledge in this area prepare the social worker to do a better job of child and family assessment a case planning.

In this workbook we present material on child development in a manner that we hope will be helpful to social workers and others wh deal with children in placement. As each stage of development is discussed, the major developmental tasks are outlined, and the chang in perceptions, abilities, and behaviour that children experience are highlighted. In addition, special developmental issues for children in placement at each stage are noted.

Throughout the book, we talk about the relationship between the child and his parents. We use the word 'parents' to mean primary caretakers who may be birth parents, foster parents, adoptive parents or other relatives.

In addition, we often use the word 'mother' to replace primary ca taker. It is true that conditions are changing and that a growing numt of fathers are taking on this primary caretaker role. However, the majority of primary caretakers still are mothers and most child development research done to date reflects this. Hence, for convenier we have sometimes used 'mother' to mean 'primary caretaker' in this text.

We hope that upon first reading you will gain information that wil be of help to you in working with at least one or two current cases in your caseload. In addition, we hope that this workbook will also stan as a reference to which you can return in the future.

This workbook has six major sections. The first five sections descri normal development in the infant, toddler, pre-school child, child between six and ten, and adolescent. In each of these sections, special issues of concern to the child in placement at that age are highlighted.

Although some comments are included in each of these sections as to ways to minimise the trauma of separation at various ages, more complete information and concrete suggestions are given in the workbook of this series entitled *Helping children when they must mot* (Fahlberg V, published *BAAF* 1982).

A section on language development from birth to age five is include in the section on the pre-school age child. At the end of Section 3 the is a listing of the usual sequences for attaining developmental milestones in the sub areas of development: personal-social, fine motor adaptive, language, and gross motor.

Section 6 summarises several special developmental issues of which workers and parents should be aware. These issues include language development, conscience development and values incorporation, temper tantrums, fears and worries, and sexual development.

Case examples and exercises have been interspersed within the text so that the reader may apply the material presented to actual cases. The exercises may be used by an individual reader or as the basis for training sessions for social workers or parents.

Exercise 1 follows. Look it over and spend some time considering two cases from your caseload, following the instructions. When you have finished reading this workbook, come back and complete Exercise 1.

*Exercise 1:*
Identifying developmental levels

Instructions

*Purpose:*

To help you learn to recognise the developmental level of children in your caseload and to plan appropriate ways of meeting their needs.

*How to do it:*

1. Think of two different children in your caseload. Select one child whom you feel has developmental delays or is 'immature'. Select a second child who is functioning at age level.

2. Using the two worksheets that follow, write a brief summary of each case. Try to include all the information specified on the worksheets.

3. As you read this workbook, keep these two cases in mind and make notes or comments in the block marked 'Indicates developmental level'.

4. After you have finished reading this workbook, answer the questions in the 'conclusions' section on the second page of the worksheets.

*Exercise 1:*
Identifying developmental levels

Worksheet 1:
'Immature child'

---

*Case summary:*

Age at time of separation (from original primary caretakers):
Present age:

---

*Observation notes:*

| Behaviour | Indicates developmental level | Normal or delayed? |
|-----------|-------------------------------|--------------------|
| 1. | | |
| 2. | | |
| 3. | | |
| 4. | | |
| 5. | | |

*Exercise 1:*
Identifying developmental levels

Worksheet 1:
'Immature child'

| Observation notes: | | |
|---|---|---|
| Behaviour | Indicates developmental level | Normal or delayed? |
| 6. | | |
| 7. | | |
| 8. | | |
| 9. | | |
| 10. | | |

*Conclusions:*

At what age level(s) do you perceive this child is functioning?

What recommendations would you give the current parental figures for meeting this child's developmental needs?

*Exercise 1:*
Identifying developmental levels

**Worksheet 2:**
'Average child'

---

*Case summary:*




Age at time of separation (from original primary caretakers):
Present age:

---

*Observation notes:*

Behaviour          Indicates developmental level        Normal or delayed?

1.

2.

3.

4.

5.

Worksheet 2:
'Average child'

*Observation notes:*

| Behaviour | Indicates developmental level | Normal or delayed? |
|-----------|-------------------------------|--------------------|
| 6. | | |
| 7. | | |
| 8. | | |
| 9. | | |
| 10. | | |

*Conclusions:*

At what age level(s) do you perceive this child is functioning?

What recommendations would you give the current parental figures for meeting this child's developmental needs?

# The first year of life

## Primary task

During the first year of life, the primary task for the baby is to build a
sense of safety and security and trust in other human beings. When a
parent wonders, 'What should I do when . . .?', the criteria for deciding
should be, 'What will help my child trust me?' The infant develops his
sense of security and trust from the day-to-day experiences he has
during the first year, not from occasional special or traumatic events.
We know it is the quality of these daily interactions between parent
and child that help the child develop physically and mentally.

Even during the first year of life it is not possible to separate a
child's innate characteristics and behaviour from the effects of the way
he is nurtured. We do know, however, that an infant deprived of
mothering will appear grossly retarded by the time he is one year old.
He may not be able to sit, stand, or walk. His vocalisation and social
interaction will be limited. He may develop 'failure to thrive'
syndrome and be unable to grow physically. If his needs for security
and affection are not met, he may not be able to give love or
incorporate social values as he matures.

## Normal development in the first year

### Physical developments

During the first year of life the child makes tremendous gains in
physical development. The rate of growth and development is so great
that parents see changes in the infant's behaviour on nearly a daily
basis. At no other time in an individual's life will his developmental
changes from month to month be so consistently noticeable.

The child's nervous system becomes organised during his first year of
life. The rate and level of this organisation seems to be related to the
quality of the relationships that the infant has with his parents. During
the first year of life the child learns to recognise and understand many
stimuli. Children learn how to learn during this first year.

In general the child gains control over his body in progression from
head to foot and from the central part of his body out to his
extremities. Thus the infant first gains voluntary control over the eye
muscles. He is first able to focus on objects eight to nine inches from
his eyes. From birth, the infant is interested in looking at the face of
his human partner. Within the first month of life most infants learn to
follow objects to the midline and within two months, 75 per cent are

following beyond the midline.

The muscles of the lower part of the face are the next to come under voluntary control. Infants smile responsively prior to three months. Next comes control over the neck muscles so that the child learns to lift his head and neck up and gains control over his head when it is held upright.

The infant then acquires large muscle control in his upper extremities so that between three and four months he can put his hands together and can use his arms for support to raise his chest up when he is lying on his stomach. In fact, near that age the child learns to roll over, first from stomach to back, and later from back to stomach. Shortly thereafter the child's head does not lag as he is pulled from a lying to a sitting position.

Between three and four months the child has enough control over his hand muscles to be able to grasp a rattle for a short period of time. By five months most children will reach for an object, and by six months will transfer objects from one hand to the other. Frequently they will put the object in their mouths in the process. At about this age the child learns to pick up small objects by use of a raking motion. Most children can use a thumb and finger grasp by the age of nine months.

By this time the child is gaining control over the large muscles in his lower extremities. He can pull himself to a standing position and can stand alone with something to hold onto. Within the next month and a half most will learn to walk holding onto furniture and will learn to stand by themselves. The child learns to stoop and recover at about the same time as he learns to walk alone. These developmental achievements usually occur at about one year of age.

By this time the child has learned to pick up small objects with a very neat, pincer-type grasp. The combination of this grasp and the mobility lead to a frustrating period for parents when the child sees and picks up every tiny thing on the floor and puts everything he has picked up into his mouth.

Language development

Language begins to emerge during the first year of life. The child *in utero* probably can hear; the newborn responds with distress to sharp sounds and prefers soft sounds. By the time the infant is three or four weeks old he turns towards sounds, and he responds most prominently to the voice of his primary caretaker. (Wolff, 1966). Vocalisations other than crying, such as coos, squeals and laughs, start during the first month of life but become more prominent in the succeeding two months.

Between six and nine months the child starts to imitate his parents' speech sounds in a non-specific fashion. By this time he is getting control over the muscles associated with his lips, tongue, and mouth. This physical fact, combined with the child's willingness to imitate, make speech development prominent at this time. For a more complete outline of language development and material on language development, see Section 3 of this workbook.

Psychological and social development
As we mentioned in the introductory section, the primary psychological task to be accomplished during the first year of life is for the child to develop a sense of trust in others. The accomplishment of this psychological task, like all other psychological tasks, is primarily a reflection of day-to-day living rather than occasional isolated experiences.

When the infant experiences discomfort and cries, a parent usually identifies and remedies the state of discomfort, and the child experiences relief. Thus, a cycle is established that teaches the child that others will meet his needs. The repeated successful completion of this cycle is critical if the child is to develop a sense of trust and security and become attached to parental figures.

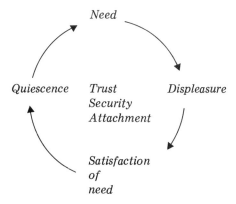

At birth, the infant does not discriminate among the various states of discomfort he experiences, and reacts in a similar way when he is afraid, angry, or in pain. Gradually, as this cycle is successfully completed on different occasions, the child becomes able to discriminate among the varying states of discomfort that he experiences and the forms of relief that alleviate the discomfort. Thus, the child begins to develop a sense of cause and effect. If the parent consistently identifies when the child is hungry and feeds him, eventually the child learns that that particular state of discomfort is alleviated by food and that the cause of the discomfort is an empty stomach.

Awareness of the effects of this cycle helps us understand why so many children who come from abusive and neglectful homes have problems with lack of trust and with identifying and correctly remedying their own body discomforts. It is not uncommon to see five or six-year-old children who were abused or neglected during the first year of life who still have difficulty differentiating when they are hungry from when they need attention.

During the first year of life normally there are fluctuations in the child's emotional responses. During the first month of life the infant getting accustomed to life outside the uterus and is often quite disorganised. However, between four and six weeks the infant becomes more stable and tends to settle into a more scheduled existence. However, periods of emotional disequilibrium and increased fussiness re-emerge for short periods around two months and between four and five months. During these periods the child often fusses for no apparent reason, and little seems to be comforting.

By age four months the infant certainly distinguishes his parents from other people. There is no doubt that the child notices moves after this time. There is a growing body of evidence that infants of one to two months distinguish their primary caretakers to varying degrees and thus would react to a move. Although children prior to six months certainly do distinguish caretakers from others, most enjoy strangers as well and do not show signs of fear or discomfort when approached by strangers.

During the early months of life the infant responds most to the particular sensations that promote contact with others. They prefer looking at the human face and listening to the human voice. They prefer the feel of soft clothing and the sense of rhythmical movement that they experience as an adult partner holds them and moves with them. Infants are especially sensitive to developing attachment behaviours during the first six months of life.

When he is between six and nine months old, the child can consistently distinguish between family members and strangers. By this age, the child begins to demonstrate fear or anxiety when he is approached by a stranger. The strength and frequency of these fear reactions increase as the child nears one year of age. This makes it increasingly difficult for the child to develop an attachment to a new primary caretaker during this period.

By the age of eight months, the child plays a more active part in trying to keep his mother close to him. The child obviously tries to catch the mother's attention. Since most children are somewhat mobile at this age, it becomes easier for them to achieve this aim. Such activity on the part of the child are a necessary part of forming an attachment and should not be discouraged. By the age of one year, the child and mother will have developed a unique pattern in terms of how they approach and respond to each other. This pattern tends to persist during the remainder of the pre-school years unless considerable effort is made to change it.

Often, we can see this pattern displayed. The baby's urge for closeness and attachment is so strong that if his mother doesn't stay close to him, he behaves in a way that tends to draw her to him. Such infants are often clingy and whiney. If the parent rejects the child at these times, the clinging and whiney behaviour increases. In these cases closeness to mother is maintained with primarily negative rather than positive interactions. If the mother shows the child that she is ready to remain close to him, he can relax and free his energies for other activities.

16

During the child's first year, attachment between mother and child normally increases, but dependency decreases. Attachment and dependency are not synonymous terms. According to Ainsworth (1952) the anxious, insecure child may falsely appear more strongly attached to his mother than the secure child who can explore fairly freely in a strange situation using his mother as a secure base. The strongly attached child may not be distressed by the appearance of a stranger. He may show awareness of his mother's absence, greet her on her return, and then resume his previous activities.

In contrast, the insecure child may not explore even when his mother is present; may become extremely alarmed by the appearance of a stranger; may seem helpless and in acute distress when his mother leaves; and on her return may seem either disinterested or in distress but in either case, incapable of making an organised attempt to reach her.

During the child's first year of life, he becomes more perceptive, takes a more active part in his relationship with his parents, and become less dependent upon them. This sets the stage for the primary tasks of the second year of life — beginning to become autonomous.

## Minimising the trauma of separation

### During the first year of life
When children change parental figures during the first year of life, it is difficult to minimise the trauma of the move as the child does not have the verbal or intellectual skills to be prepared ahead of time. Our only avenues for smoothing the way involve active transferring of the parenting from the former primary caretaker to the 'new' caretaker. This is especially difficult to accomplish when children come into care. Changes in basic daily routines should be kept to a minimum if possible. The new parental figures need to understand how and why the child's basic trust may be undermined by a move at this time, and be willing to focus on rebuilding trust for adults after the move.

Many children who come into care during the first year of life have not yet had the opportunity to learn to trust parental figures. In such cases the new parental figures will have this as their major task.

## Effects of separation from, or loss of, parental objects during the first year of life

Even before the child reaches the age at which he is obviously anxious about strangers, he is affected by moves from one home to another. He no doubt is aware of changes in rhythm and routine that occur with a move. The child reacts to the differences in temperature, noise, and visual stimulation that vary from household to household. He may lose his sense of being able to rely on the environment and the individuals within it.

Interruptions in parenting will interrupt the child's process of sorting out his perceptions of the world. Since precursors to logical thinking and basic cause and effect reasoning begin even at this young age, w may see disturbances in this area. Children who have been asked to adjust to varying routines and environments during infancy may ha their sense of security upset enough that they may become less flex in the future.

During the latter half of the first year the psychological tasks are increase recognition and awareness, to differentiate primary caretak from strangers, and to increase reciprocity and mutuality in terms o inter-personal relationships. Loss of parental figures during this stag of development is likely to lead to problems in terms of trusting caretakers and in terms of social interactions.

In Exercise 2 on the next page, you have an opportunity to ident a child's developmental levels and needs during infancy.

*Exercise 2:*
Identifying developmental needs in the infant

Instructions

*Purpose:*

To help you learn to identify developmental levels and needs of infants so that appropriate foster care placements may be selected.

*How to do it:*

1. Read Jason's case history.

2. Answer the questions on the next page and then compare your own answers with those of another caseworker on the sample worksheet.

Jason's case

*Jason is a 13-month-old who has just come into care. His mother is 18 years old. The father left the family when Jason was one month old. His mother frequently leaves Jason alone for several hours in the evening while she goes out with friends. During the day the mother spends most of her time watching television. She rarely holds Jason; she props his bottle. Little verbal or physical stimulation for Jason has come from his mother.*

*Jason is below the third percentile in height and weight and has poor muscle tone. He spends most of his time lying passively, rarely moving or vocalising. Jason does not yet drink from a cup. He can, but rarely does, roll over. He sits unsupported for just a minute or two and then topples forward. Jason will momentarily hold a rattle but shows no active interest in it. He rarely cries and never laughs or squeals.*

Worksheet

1. At what developmental level(s) does Jason seem to be functioning?

2. What type of foster home would you select for Jason?

3. What type of advice would you give to the foster parents in terms of meeting Jason's developmental needs?

*Exercise 2:*
Identifying developmental needs in the infant

**Sample worksheet**

1. At what developmental level(s) does Jason seem to be functioning?

   At about the level of a three to four month old baby but his vocalisation is underdeveloped even for this age.

2. What type of foster home would you select for Jason?

   Where there is a foster-mother who likes and is experienced with babies, who has time to give a lot of attention to Jason, and who can understand that some babies need special attention to help them catch up on their chronological age.

3. What type of advice would you give to the foster parents in terms of meeting Jason's developmental needs?

   An explanation of the level at which he is functioning, of the need to treat him first as a very young baby, to help him develop security and trust but also give him lots of stimulation, attention and physical contact to help him 'catch up'.

## The primary task

The overriding task for the child from one to three years is to separate psychologically from his mother and to begin to develop self confidence and self esteem. When faced with a 'What should I do when . . .?' question about a child of this age, the criteria for deciding should be, 'What will make my child feel more capable?' Although the urge for autonomy exists from the time the child is mobile, it becomes most evident between the ages of one year and two and a half.

## Normal development

At about 12 months when the child stands and walks, his perspective on the world changes literally and figuratively. As the child begins to walk, he develops the capacity to pick up very small objects. As a result he is eminently capable of 'getting into things' as he exploits his two newly acquired skills. The typical child at 12 months is very social. In a secure setting, he may even seem to be somewhat indiscriminate in giving affection as he smiles and talks with everyone.

Although we speak of the 'terrible twos', the period we are referring to usually extends from 18 to 30 months. The toddler goes through a normal oppositional, stubborn, egocentric stage that is necessary to the development of his identity. In fact, it has been found that those children who do not go through the normal oppositional stage are more dependent later on in life.

During the second year of life the toddler does not get on as well with others as he did previously. He does not seem to be in good emotional equilibrium. He becomes demanding, assertive, and independent. He is impulsive and has a short attention span. He becomes easily frustrated and is prone to temper tantrums.

When he is between 12 and 18 months old, the child typically becomes apprehensive about being physically separated from his mother. Toddlers tend to be constantly underfoot as they cling to their parents. This relates to the fact that the developmental task for the toddler is psychological separation and individuation. When his mother is physically absent, the toddler feels out of control of the situation and becomes more anxious and apprehensive. As the toddler loses sight of mother and then finds her again, he is learning about himself as an individual. He uses his mother as a safe base from which to explore the world.

22

Prominent words in the vocabulary of an 18-month-old are 'me', 'mine', and 'no'. These words support his emerging autonomy. The child begins to distinguish between 'you' and 'me'; he starts to separate his own identity from his mother's. Games such as 'Point to your nose: point to my mouth', help him learn this type of differentiation.

The 18-month-old is very egocentric. He does not yet perceive other people as individuals like himself. The child's defiance and resistance in this period are not so much aggressive as self-protective. He is trying to establish himself in the world.

We can see the toddler begin to internalise the values of others during this period. As the toddler approaches an object the parents don't want him to touch, they say 'no' in a firm voice and may accompany this with a smack on the offending hand. Later, as the child approaches this object he himself says 'no, no', but he cannot yet quite stop himself from touching. He needs mother's reinforcing 'That's right; that is a no-no.' However, shortly thereafter the child will reach out to touch this object saying 'no, no' and then quickly withdraw his own hand or he will even give himself a smack. This is the very beginning stage of incorporation of values and is, as such, a precursor to conscience development.

As the toddler reaches two years of age, his ability to perceive things and to imitate behaviour have become more developed. He loves to mimic his parents and to 'help' them with household tasks. He cooperates better with dressing himself, although he can usually take off more garments than he can put on. The child of this age will play alone or play in a parallel fashion with other children. He is still 'selfish' and not ready to share.

The two-year-old toddler still does not fully accept his mother as a separate individual. He alternates between being dependent and being self-contained. The resurgence of fear toward strangers that occurs at 18 months subsides.

He is capable of showing a wide variety of feelings — frustration, anger, sadness, fear, and affection. He also shows signs of pity, sympathy, modesty, and shame. Two-year-olds can be most touching when they try to comfort an upset parent with 'poor mummy' or 'poor daddy'. The two-year-old is aware of praise, and smiles when he hears it. He may even praise himself with statements such as 'good job.'

Between two and three years, the child goes through a period where extremes are the norm. He is either very dependent or very independent, and his mood changes from hour to hour. He is extremely aggressive or extremely withdrawn; very helpful or very stubborn. He is now steady on his feet; his vocabulary grows by leaps and bounds. Toilet training becomes feasible and, for most children, day-time training is completed by the third birthday.

## Parents' role with toddlers

What kind of environment helps the child attain the psychological tasks at hand for these two years? The toddler needs parents who can give encouragement without pressure for the development of new skills, who help him feel 'big' and capable. In addition, it is the parents' responsibility to provide for the child's safety and wellbeing. Change in the environment can do much to prevent accidents and to promote healthy parent-child relationships.

In order to protect the toddler, cleaning materials, medicines, and poisons must be kept in inaccessible places. Inaccessible places get harder to find during this period as the child learns to climb up on a chair to get desirable objects. Until the child learns to manage stairs, most parents use gates to block them off.

Late during this period the child learns to turn a door knob to open the door, so until then keeping certain rooms of the house closed off a sensible safety precaution. After these kinds of practical changes are made in the environment, enough 'nos' invariably remain to provide the child with ample opposition for growth.

The child's short attention span and distractability are the parents' principal allies during this period. Substituting a safe toy for a forbidden one usually works. Reasoning does not. Although a quick t on an offending hand or a single smack on the bottom may help to reinforce verbal requests, repeated harsh physical punishment does no help psychological development.

If the parents perceive the normal negativism of the toddler age as personal attack and get into repeated win-lose battles, they may well be in for difficulties with the child later on. Through such conflicts the child learns to behave as though his integrity as a person is in danger if he submits to even the smallest demands of another. Resistance and conflict, rather than mutuality, become the primary mode of interaction between such parents and children.

Children of this age are creatures of routine. Changes in routine or abrupt transitions usually result in a child who is more easily frustrated and upset than normal. All mothers have had the experience of disrupting their child's usual nap routine to take them for an afternoon appointment, and all mothers have learned that they 'pay' for this change in routine for the remainder of the day.

A special note should be made about the child's difficulty in following his mother until about the age of three. The toddler has difficulty in moving toward a *moving* object. This should not be interpreted as 'naughty' or resistant behaviour. Usually the mother must transport the child by buggy, grocery trolley, or in her arms. When mother and toddler are out for a pleasure walk, it is common to see the mother walk a short distance, remain stationary until her child catches up with her, and then repeat this sequence.

## Toddlers in placement

In this section, three issues are highlighted because of the particular need for workers to be keyed into them. The first is the expression of assertion and anger during these stages. It is particularly important for workers to be able to help birth parents, foster parents, and others interpret the child's development in the expression of assertion and anger, for it is this behaviour that will concern all of them and will be brought to the attention of the worker. For similar reasons, toilet training is highlighted here. Finally, the developmental effects of separation are noted here so that workers can help avoid, identify, and work through these reactions.

Assertion and anger

As the toddler gains in independence, his anger is aroused chiefly by interference with his physical activity. By 21 months, frustration may also stem from the toddler's inadequate ability to express his wants and needs.

When the 18-month-old is angry, he is apt to have a tantrum, crying intensely and throwing himself on the floor. He may also hit, kick, and struggle if an adult tries to control him. The toddler of this age tends to be rough with animals and with younger children. He is apt to pull hair and to hug too tightly.

Typically, the two-year-old is not as aggressive as the one and a half year old. However, he may hit, poke, or bite other children. He is into the ownership stage and will engage in a tug-of-war over toys and other objects. Although he may 'mess up' the house, generally he is not destructive.

By age two and a half he has become more destructive, and he is more aggressive both with other children and with adults. He attacks other children with the intent to hurt, usually in disputes over toys.

Without warning he may walk up and hit a stranger. He may, again, have kicking, hitting, and head-banging type tantrums.

Toilet training

Toilet training cannot occur until the child becomes aware of the sensations of a full bladder and a full bowel. Many mothers learn to identify the signals of an impending bowel movement and place the infant or toddler on the pot just in time; however, this is not true toilet training.

Commonly toddlers first become aware of wet or full pants immediately after they occur rather than before, much to the frustration of the parents. However, this is a necessary stage, for until the child becomes aware of the discomfort *after* it occurs, he cannot become aware of the full sensation prior to urinating or defecating. Children who have a low sensitivity to skin sensations may be delayed in terms of toilet training.

It is also quite common for children to 'go' just after they get off the potty rather than while they are on it. Again, although this is very frustrating to parents it indicates that the child is beginning to relate the potty to going to the bathroom; he just has not yet mastered the proper sequence.

It is very difficult to toilet train a child who is wearing nappies. Switching to training pants is necessary to complete toilet training in regard to urination. Many children are quite regular in terms of the time of day that they have their bowel movements, and so it is easier for mother to put the child on the potty at the appropriate time.

Since children at this age tend to be stubborn and messy, parents often attribute difficulties in toilet training to the child's stubbornness. However, with most children this is not true initially.

However, if parents make a control issue out of toilet training or use harsh disciplinary techniques, then the stubbornness of this age may extend to toilet training as well. This is not likely to happen if th parents are relaxed but helpful about teaching toileting skills.

One of the most frustrating events for parents is when the child has a bowel movement during a nap or early in the morning and expresses his messiness by smearing and playing with the feces. The child does not know that this is wrong. Rather, it fits with the toddler's strong urges to explore and mess with anything he can get his hands on.

## Minimising the trauma of separation

### The toddler years

It is important that toddlers be prepared for moves by adequate pre-placement preparation if at all possible. If the move gives the toddler the message 'strangers may come and take you away from parents anytime and without parental permission', long-range, chronic worries and fears are likely, as well as lack of trust for parental figures to be able to keep children safe and secure.

The goal during the moving process should be to transfer attachment from the previous caretakers to the new caretakers as much as possible. This means that the two sets of parents need to have contact and that the 'old' parents need actively to transfer the day-to-day caretaking tasks to the 'new' parents, thus giving the toddler permission to take from the new parental figures (*Helping children when they must move*, Fahlberg).

Because memories of this age are later triggered by similar emotions or by events similar to those occurring near the time of a move, we must be very alert to noting *all* events surrounding the move on a permanent record which will accompany the child. Such records can be invaluable in helping both the child and subsequent parental figures understand the child's reaction to various events in his life.

### Case example
*Eight-year-old Peter had difficulty on trips to the grocery store with his adoptive mother. He seemed to 'fuzz out' at these times and be unaware of his surroundings. He would wander off in the store as though he were in a daze. Such behaviour was not evident in other situations. The adoptive parents were very confused by Peter's behaviour and decided perhaps they just shouldn't take him to the stores. They mentioned this behaviour to their social worker, who, in looking through the record, learned that Peter had come into care at the age of two in rather unusual circumstances. His family had been*

*well known to the child care staff and to the police because of frequent bouts of family violence.*

*Following one such episode, when the police and social worker went to the house, a relative threatened to harm them both. Peter's mother told them that if they left she would immediately bring Peter to them at the corner car park so that he could be admitted to care. The car park was that of a large grocery store.*

*Subsequently trips to the grocery store triggered memories of the first move on an unconscious basis and triggered Peter's feelings of loss and confusion that accompanied his initial separation from his birth family. Once Peter and his adoptive parents understood the root of his behaviour at the store, they could work together on helping him learn that grocery stores need not be associated with loss.*

Post-placement contacts with previous caretakers are important to the toddler. If they do not occur, it is common that the child will, at the age of four to five, think that the previous parental figures are dead. Pictures of past families make it possible for subsequent work to be done on separation issues once the child is old enough verbally and cognitively to deal with these feelings. If a child moves during the toddler years, it is nearly certain that he will need help as he matures in understanding the reasons for the move.

## Effects of separation or loss on the toddler

Separations at this stage of development tend strongly to affect the development of the child's autonomy. Children who experience losses at this age may have problems in developing an appropriate balance between dependency and autonomy.

Some children with separation or loss experiences will become very dependent and clingy. Such children are usually afraid to show age-appropriate autonomy. Since they do not trust that adults will be there when they need them, they insist on keeping adults constantly in sight by demanding or clinging.

Other children who have experienced separation from or loss of attachment figures at this age may go to the opposite extreme and become too autonomous. Such a child is apt to parent himself. He withholds affection and may seem stubborn and resistant.

Such developmental reactions to separation and losses are not necessarily of short duration. Frequently, if not recognised and remedied, these reactions persist for years. It is not uncommon to see nine, ten, and eleven-year-old children in foster care who are still constantly clinging in spite of numerous attempts to break them of this habit. Other children show the effects of extreme autonomy through secondary school years and adolescence.

Underlying both these reactions is a lack of trust for others. The first is a 'I can't count on you wanting to stay close so I will have to keep an eye on you' response; the second is 'I can't count on you being close when I need you, so I will have to count on myself'.

27

Since these problems are frequent for children in care, social work and foster parents need to be aware of the conflict between dependency and independency that characterises this age period. If there have been interruptions in the child's caretaking during this period, then his later experiences must provide him with opportunities for increasing trust and for increasing age-appropriate autonomy. It must be recognised that the child's effort to control his environment a healthy coping mechanism that must be kept in proportion so that i works for the child instead of against him. Exercise 3 asks you to explore these issues.

*Exercise 3:*
**Identifying unmet dependency needs and dealing with the behavioural regression in such cases**

Instructions

*Purpose:*

To help you learn to identify a child's unmet dependency needs and to plan to meet them.

*How to do it:*

1. Read Joshua's case history.

2. Answer the questions on the next page and then compare your own answers with those of another caseworker on the sample worksheet.

### Joshua's case

*Joshua is five. He has been in and out of foster care since he was two because of repeated episodes of neglect by his mother and physical abuse by several of her boyfriends. In the foster home there is an infant and two toddlers. Occasionally, the foster mum finds Joshua sitting under the desk, rocking and sucking on a baby bottle he has take taken from a younger child.*

*At bedtime Joshua rocks himself in the bed until he falls asleep. He continually grabs the toddlers' toys from them and seems to prefer playing with such toys rather than with toys more appropriate for his age. Sometimes he speaks very clearly; at other times he uses 'baby talk.'*

*Exercise 3:*
Identifying unmet dependency needs and dealing with the behaviour
regression in such cases

## Worksheet

1. What unmet dependency needs does Joshua appear to have?

2. How would you explain his problems from a developmental standpoint
   to the foster parents?

3. What suggestions do you have for the foster parents to meet Joshua's
   unmet needs so that they will not persist later in his life?

*Exercise 3:*
Identifying unmet dependency needs and dealing with the behavioural regression in such cases

Sample worksheet

---

1. What unmet dependency needs does Joshua appear to have?

   He has not been given consistency and reliability or been able to develop a sense of trust because of the repeated separations and neglect.

---

2. How would you explain his problems from a developmental standpoint to the foster parents?

   He has not been able to go through the normal toddler stages of alternating between dependency and becoming more autonomous and he has not developed a sense of trust.

---

3. What suggestions do you have for the foster parents to meet Joshua's unmet needs so that they will not persist later in his life?

   They need to allow him to be dependent and develop trust by explaining absences and separations, showing affection especially at bed time and giving him a lot of individual attention. At the same time they need to praise and encourage him for any new achievements. They should talk to him about his past and be aware of what triggers off feelings of loss and confusion.

# The pre-school years

## The primary tasks

The pre-school years are when proficiency in self care within the home setting is attained: this is the period of questions; the time of play and continuing individuation and independence for the child.

## Normal development

By age three the child's need to be physically near his mother is no longer so urgent. A three-year-old can feel secure away from his mother in a strange place if he is with people that he got to know while in her presence. Sensitivity to this is a very important consideration when moving children into foster or adoptive placements.

In general the three-year-old seems to be in good equilibrium. He is usually happy and contented; he enjoys play by himself; he seems to have achieved some measure of emotional and physical self control. He is generally friendly and helpful. He has learned to help dress and undress himself and, although he may have occasional accidents, he usually does not need nappies in the daytime.

The three-year-old's readiness to conform to the spoken word is one of his outstanding characteristics. It is possible to bargain with a three-year-old — 'You do this, and I'll do that for you.' He has this capacity because he realises he is a separate person from others. While bargaining works, reasoning does not yet. Reasoning requires more conceptual skills than the three-year-old usually has. Distraction is still a useful disciplinary technique.

In general, the three-year-old is less rebellious than he was at two. When he does resist, he uses language rather than biting, scratching, or kicking. He enjoys both gross and fine motor activities. A three-year-old begins to take turns — the first kind of sharing.

Three-year-olds frequently ask questions to which they know the answers. This behaviour is, in part, an effort to find out which information is consistent and which inconsistent. From the child's point of view, the world is a very confusing place. Some perceptions seems consistent; others do not. For example, what is acceptable behaviour at one time may not be acceptable at a different time or in another setting. Loud, boisterous play may be all right at certain times of the day, but not when parents are trying to sleep or a baby is napping.

The three-year-old is capable of prolonged anxiety and jealousy. His greatest fear is one of abandonment. As the child turns four, some of his two-year-old stubbornness re-emerges; however, this stubbornness seems 'softer' and frequently has a playful quality about it. The four-year-old enjoys silly talk, silly names, silly rhyming, silly showing off.

Four-year-olds tend to be afraid of the dark. Often a night-light solves many bedtime problems. They may fear strange noises. The four-year-old enjoys being somewhat scared by the adult in play; he will run and scream and then ask the adult to 'do it again'.

The typical four-year-old is likely to return to some physical aggression while continuing to be verbally aggressive. He engages in name calling and bragging. He plays in a group and may aggressively exclude others from it.

He is talkative and gives long explanations in answer to parental questions. When he misbehaves, he is prone to blame others or deny his involvement. He may behave badly on purpose in order to get a reaction. The four-year-old is able to focus on similarities and differences. His questions reflect his efforts to conceptualise and to order his experience rather than just a hunger for information. Most of his questions are of the 'how?' and 'why?' type.

The four-year-old loves dramatic, imaginative play. Although he is able to dress and undress himself with little assistance, he frequently enjoys help as a form of nurturing. He begins to have a sense of past and a sense of future. When told 'in a little while' or 'in half an hour', he wants to know how long that is.

The child at five seems to be in a good state of equilibrium; his perceptions and his abilities seem to mesh. Five is an age of self containment and independence. In general the five-year-old is more serious and realistic than he was earlier or will become later. He is oriented to the here and now.

His childish way of speaking disappears. The five-year-old is curious and eager for information; however, his questions are fewer and more relevant. His ability to have a genuine exchange of ideas is limited. He has trouble suppressing himself even momentarily and will interrupt frequently.

The five-year-old enjoys brief separations from his home and his mother. He is friendly and talks to everyone. This is not to be confused with indiscriminate affection, which involves more than talk. A vein of politeness and tact is emerging. There is also an emerging sense of shame and a sense of status.

The five-year-old is aware of being different from others, and of differences in others. He becomes increasingly aware of differences between the sexes.

When the child of five paints or draws, the idea precedes the production, rather than the reverse as occurred when he was four. His drawings and dramatic play are more realistic.

The five-year-old is not as fearful as the four-year-old. His fear of imaginary things slackens because he is so reality-oriented. However, he may be fearful of being far from his parents in the dark.

Bargaining continues to work as a disciplinary technique. If the five-year-old feels stress, he increases his activity level. Since he frequently becomes hyperactive under stress, some form of 'time out' procedure may help him regain his equilibrium. Distraction does not work as well as at earlier ages.

## Minimising the trauma of moves

### The pre-school years

Because of the prominence of magical thinking and continued egocentricity, it is very important that everyone involved in moving the pre-school age child be on the alert for the child's misperception as to the reasons for the move and for his particular brand of magical thinking.

Because the pre-school child tends to act out his concerns through play, parental figures need to pay close attention to the child's verbalisations during play as this frequently gives clues as to misperceptions. Parental figures, both before and after the move, should note down any odd or peculiar statements that the child mak and share them with the social worker. Such statements if looked at carefully, frequently give clues as to the child's particular piece of magical thinking. We cannot correct the child's misperceptions and/o magical thinking unless we first identify them. Further suggestions o minimising the trauma of moves at this age are given in the workbook of this series entitled *Helping children when they must move* (Fahlbe 1982).

## The pre-school child in placement

Again, a few developmental issues are highlighted here that are particularly important for workers and parents of children in placeme

Because delays in language development are the most common developmental delay seen in the abused and/or neglected child, (Elme and Gregg 1967) we are including a brief synopsis of normal language development during the first five years, so that those involved with children can identify those children with speech delays at an early age

Assertion and anger in the pre-school child are highlighted here to help workers and parents separate disturbing but normal behaviour from that which may indicate a more serious problem. Similarly, normal development in relation to dependency and autonomy is discussed so that behaviour on this dimension can be more intelligentl interpreted by worker and parent.

This section also includes a discussion of the pre-school child's propensity for magical thinking, and his need to resolve oedipal issues. Both of these areas may pose problems for the child who is separated from his parents in his pre-school years.

Following Exercise 4 at the end of this section there is a series of charts which outline the normal progression of development from birt to the age of five. These charts include personal-social; fine-motor adaptive; gross motor and language development.

## Language development

Language delays are common among children in placement. This section contains a brief synopsis of normal language development during the first five years so that those involved with children can identify those children with speech delays at an early age.

Language development is essential because it makes possible the higher mental processes that allow humans to attain self-control and to delay gratification of urges. It gives children a way to express their feelings other than by acting them out. It also makes memory possible. A child's memories of the time before he could speak are scanty and are usually stored either as visual images or as feelings.

## At infancy

From birth on, infants react adversely to loud sharp sounds. At about three weeks they start to respond positively to soft sounds, especially the human voice. Even before they are four months old, infants make a variety of sounds; they babble, coo, chuckle, gurgle, and laugh. Even early in infancy, children are very responsive to the human voice and their vocalisations increase when someone talks or plays with them.

Midway through the first year of life, infants begin to make vowel and consonant sounds and even put some sounds together into syllables. Within another month or so they begin to imitate speech sounds.

By age one most children are using 'mama' and 'dada' and have two or three other words in their vocabularies. They jabber a lot. They respond to their own names, to 'no, no' and to 'give it to me.' By 18 months most children have a vocabulary of about ten words (Gessel *et al* 1940). They can say 'no' and may use the pronouns 'me' and 'mine'. They are using words to replace or accompany gestures.

At two most children combine words into phrases or short sentences. Their jargon has almost disappeared. They use nouns more than other parts of speech. The vocabulary of the average two-year-old is about 300 words. (Gesell *et al* 1940). Most can name some animals, objects, and parts of the body. They will usually try to imitate any single words said to them. Pronouns come into use during the period between 18 and 30 months, usually emerging in this order: 'mine', 'me', 'you', and 'I'. At two most children are still prone to calling themselves by their given names — 'Billy wants a cookie.' The rhythm of the typical two-year-old's voice is sing-song, and he may often echo what others say.

Between the ages of two and three, the child begins to add 's' to words to make plurals. He learns to use the words he acquired earlier in sentences. He uses nouns, pronouns, verbs, and some adjectives. He begins to understand prepositions although he can't use them. His vocabulary increases to over 1,000 words. (Gesell *et al* 1946). He uses words to resist and to ask questions.

## At four

At four the child uses questions to order his experience and to begin
to conceptualise and group things. 'Why' and 'how' introduce his
frequent questions. He can count by rote. He learns to use prepositic
As adverbs become evident in his language, he has mastered all parts
speech. Conversation no longer interferes with his eating. He has
learned the names of colours.

By age five, the child's language is essentially complete in structur
and form. He loses his infant articulation; he sounds grown up now.
Usually by five, the melody and rhythm of his speech are smooth as
well. The most common articulation errors at this age are substitutin
an 'f' or 'd' for 'th'; softening 'r' until it sounds like 'w'; and
substituting 'w' for 'l'.

The five-year-old has acquired an ear for detail; he is able to ask tl
meaning of single words, rather than asking what an entire sentence
means. He has difficulty suppressing his own view even temporarily;
thus genuine interchange of ideas remains limited. In 'show and tell'
type activities, he is interested in doing the showing and telling rathe
than the listening.

## Assertion and anger

By age three the pre-school child has gained increased self-control an
exhibits less aggression. Increased use of language allows him to expr
his wants and desires so that he is not so easily frustrated, and
vocalisation may be used to express anger and frustration when it
occurs. Anger is now aroused less by interference with physical activi
and more by interference with his possessions or with his plans. The
child commonly uses verbal threats to assert himself and express ange

Age four with its return of stubbornness is accompanied by a retur
to physically aggressive behaviour. Biting, hitting, kicking, and throw
things are not uncommon in the four-year-old. In addition four is
verbally aggressive and may use name calling, bragging and boasting to
assert himself. He tends to be rough and careless with toys and may
aggressively exclude others from the group.

Five, as mentioned earlier tends to be an age of equilibrium which
means that the child is exposed to less frustration and we see less
aggression. When angry, five may stamp his feet or slam the door. 'I
hate you' or 'I wish you were dead' are common verbal expressions of
anger for both the four and five-year old.

## Dependency and autonomy

Three, four, and five-year olds use intellectual powers and imaginative
skills as they play. Through play they continue to work on the balanc
between dependency and autonomy. Thus we see two recurring theme
in play (Hymes, 1969).

On the one hand the pre-school child loves to play at being baby. H
may choose to take on the role of the weak, helpless, and defenceless.
This occurs when he takes the role of the baby while playing house, or
the sick person while playing doctor, or the prisoner when playing cop

and robbers, or cowboys and indians. When he takes on this helpless babyish role, he may want to rock, suck from a bottle, or get into a cot. He is likely to want to play under tables or to construct a cosy corner or 'tent' for this type of play.

The second kind of play involves being big, strong, and bossy. When the child engages in play this way, he wants to be the mother or father, the teacher, the doctor, or the policeman. When he takes on these roles, he is likely to be very bossy, even tyrannical.

His play reflects his feelings and his thoughts, not his experiences. Foster parents and social workers sometimes assume that the child playing out a 'big' role is reflecting the type of parenting he has experienced in the past rather than expressing a developmental need to feel 'big' and in control of things.

### Magical thinking

As part of ego development each individual must come to grips with integrating the 'good' and the 'bad' in himself. One of the ways that a child does this is by developing imaginary friends. The imaginary playmates are frequently blamed for anything that the child does wrong wrong. All the 'bad' in the child is attributed to the imaginary friend. Or, sometimes the imaginary friend becomes the personalisation of the scared, dependent, little aspect of the child. Thus, a pre-school child may say '*I'm* not afraid of the dark but Sammie is. You'd better leave on the light or he may be scared and cry, and then *I* couldn't sleep.'

### Case example: Johnnie

*Johnnie is a four-year-old who was placed for adoption when he was nearly three. In spite of firm recommendations to the contrary, his adoptive parents changed his name from Gerald to Johnnie. In the six months he was in adoption placement, Johnnie developed a series of behavioural problems and did not measure up to the adoptive parents' expectations. He was reprimanded each time he referred to himself as Gerald.*

*The adoption disrupted, and Johnnie was again placed in foster care. He was adamant that his name was Johnnie. He was upset when his foster parents tried to use his original name of Gerald, although Johnnie had been his name for only an eighth of his lifetime. In foster care Johnnie was 'too good.' He seemed very apprehensive about making any mistakes, or any messes, or about asserting his autonomy in any way.*

*In an attempt to determine the nature of his conflict about the name Johnnie's social worker compiled a Life Story. She showed him pictures of himself as an infant, and identified those pictures as Gerald. When she got to the part about the adoptive placement, she talked of the name change to Johnnie. She then talked about Johnnie's experience in the adoptive home and his return to foster care. She explained that Gerald and Johnnie are really one person. At this point Johnnie became agitated and repeatedly said, 'Gerry is a bad boy; he's naughty;*

*I'm Johnnie.'*

*It was clear that Johnnie was going through the normal 'good bo{ versus 'bad boy' conflict that each pre-school child has to resolve. However, for Johnnie the name change became associated with the split between good and bad. To this little boy, Gerry signified the 'b child' who had to move from the foster home to an adoptive home c who did not measure up. Johnnie was the 'good' child; however, he not done a 'good enough' job of being Johnnie in the adoptive home and thus had to leave. Back in foster care he was doing his best to be the 'good' Johnnie so he would not have to move again.*

Pre-school children are egocentric and prone to 'magical thinking'. Magical thinking includes the idea that 'wishes come true'. Many pre school children feel guilty about their thoughts, wishes or desires. M( gradually find out that their wishes do not make things come true. However, the wishes that all pre-school children have sometimes suck 'I don't like you and I wish you weren't my mummy any more; or 'I want to have a new family instead of you; or 'I wish you were dead' have 'come true' for children who have been moved into placement. this happens, then the magical thinking is reinforced and is apt to persist long beyond the common age for it to subside.

Children who lose a parent through any means — death, divorce, o placement in care — tend to blame themselves for the events in their life. They feel this way both because of their egocentricity and becau of magical thinking. If parents are sensitive about magical thinking, they may help the child understand what he is doing and keep his behaviour from continuing beyond the age at which it is appropriate.

## Case example: Suzanna

*Suzanna was a child of six whose mother had died after a long lingeri illness when Suzanna was four. During the course of her mother's illness, Suzanna was frequently separated from her; she became angry about these separations and, on occasion, wished that her mother would die. Suzanna's father remarried. She and her step-mother had many difficulties in their relationship. The behaviour that upset the step-mother most was what she called 'the look.' She had learned that when the day started out with 'the look', it rapidly progressed to one negative interaction after the other. The step-mother felt that on thos days nothing she did mattered. She was quite certain that if, in the course of therapy, we could get rid of 'the look' many of their problems would disappear.*

*Initially I was quite sceptical of the mother's perceptions in this case. However, in the course of therapy, one day Suzanna became ver} upset with me, and she gave me 'the look'. Once I saw it, I recognised as an attempted spell. As a result of her experiences when she was fou Suzanna feared that her wishes made things come true. From her perception it had happened once, and it might happen again. If she an her step-mother got off to a bad start in the morning, Suzanna would*

38

*put a 'spell' on her before she left home. She then, of course, lived in fear all day that it might come true.*

*Being preoccupied with that mixed wish-fear, she would have a bad day at school and a bad day with her step-mother when she came home. Suzanna's greatest fear was that she might be a witch. This fear was heightened by the consistency with which a bad day followed 'the look', and her step-mother's fear of it.*

### Oedipal issues

During this same age span the child is going through the Oedipal stage. During the Oedipal stage the child competes with the parent of the same sex for the attention of the parent of the opposite sex. It is not uncommon for the pre-school age boy to say 'When I grow up I am going to marry mummy' or for the girl to make a similar declaration with regard to her dad.

However, the child soon starts to realise that to get the exclusive attention of the parent of the opposite sex something must first happen to the parent of the same sex. The pre-school child is faced with a dilemma. The parent he wants 'to get rid of' is also an important love object. To win means that he will lose as well. There is also guilt associated with these thoughts of getting rid of the parent of the same sex.

In addition, the magical thinking that is so prominent at this age increases the child's fears that something may happen to the parent of the same sex because the child has wished to eliminate that parent. The child may act out in order to be punished. If the punishment occurs at the hands of the parent of the same sex and is extreme, the child's fears of retaliation for his 'bad' thoughts are reinforced. If the discipline is appropriate and fair, then the child's guilts and fears will more likely subside. If through death, or foster care placement, the child loses the parent of the same sex, the child becomes increasingly frightened of his own omnipotence.

The child may also view loss of the parent of the opposite sex as punishment for 'bad' thoughts. The child may even think that the parent of the same sex was losing the battle and decides 'If I can't have him/her then no one can.' At any rate loss of or separations from parents during this critical stage in development may lead to long-lasting problems with sexual identification or to the persistence of the magical thinking into later years.

Sometimes parents who do not have a satisfying marital relationship behave in ways that increase the Oedipal problems. For example, a mother who is not receiving much attention from her husband may become over involved with her young son and focus all of her attention on him. Or, a mother who is lonely may take her son to bed with her whenever dad is out of town or working nights. Such behaviour on the part of the parents may increase the child's fears of retaliation if the other parent finds out what is happening.

Again, because of magical thinking, children may inappropriately attribute cause and effect. Children are very likely to blame themselves

39

for everything bad that happens to them or to their family. Such bla
has frequently been reinforced by parental statements that imply th.
all the parent's problems are the child's fault. Such statements as 'H
will be the death of me yet' or 'If you aren't good, you'll be sorry' a
tend to reinforce the child's sense of responsibility for all that happe

In Exercise 4 that follows, you have an opportunity to identify
Merrilee's needs and to describe how you would create an environme
in which a pre-school child could exert her urges for autonomy and s
have her dependency needs met.

*Exercise 4:*

Identifying the needs of the pre-school child and creating an environment to meet the needs for appropriate autonomy

Instructions

*Purpose:*

To help identify ways in which children have had their urge for autonomy undermined by moves during this stage of development.

To outline ways that would be appropriate for the pre-school child to exert his or her urges for autonomy while at the same time meeting the child's dependency needs.

*How to do it:*

1. Read Merrilee's case history that begins on the following page. (see also *Helping children when they must move,* Fahlberg 1982).

2. Answer the questions on the worksheet and then compare your own answers with those of another caseworker on the sample worksheet.

## Merrilee's case

Merrilee lived with her birth mother until she was sixteen months old. During Merrilee's first year, her mother had been reported for neglec. It was not too serious, and Merrilee remained in the home. When Merrilee was fourteen months old, her mother gave birth to a baby bo and after that, began to neglect her more seriously. Merrilee came int care while her baby brother remained with the mother. Later he, too, came into care although in a different home.

When Merrilee came into foster care, the agency staff felt that it would be too confusing for her to see her birth mother. The worker recommended an 'adjustment period' for both mother and child with no visits. After this initial adjustment period, both Merrilee and her birth mother seemed to have 'adjusted' so well to the separation that both the mother and worker were reluctant to initiate contact betwee the two. The mother relinquished her rights after six months, never having seen Merrilee again.

Merrilee was a bright and precocious child who became a valued member of the foster family. The foster family wanted to adopt Merrilee; however, the agency was reluctant to allow this. They opposed foster parent adoption in general. In addition, they were concerned about confidentiality because the foster parents knew who the birth mother was. However, the foster parents had had an application in for some time to adopt an infant. Soon after Merrilee's placement with the foster family, an infant boy became available for adoption through a private agency. This boy was placed for adoption with the foster parents, and another adoptive family was sought for Merrilee.

An adoptive family who lived 350 miles away was selected. The initial placement was that the adoptive family would come and pick up Merrilee at the social services department and take her for an all-da outing. They planned to return her to the social services department s that her worker could take her to her foster home for her last night there. The following day the foster mother was to bring her into the agency; the adoptive family would then take her to their home. There was no plan for the foster and adoptive parents to meet.

This first visit, an all-day outing, went very well, as first visits frequently do. The adoptive family asked Merrilee if she would like to spend the night with them and she said yes. They called the social worker who agreed with the change in plan. The following morning, the adoptive parents brought Merrilee back to the agency to say her final good-bye to her foster mother. Her foster father who was at work and who knew that he would be upset by the separation, said his 'good-byes' to Merrilee over the phone. The worker took her from the room with her adoptive parents to a room down the hall. Her foster mother was waiting there to give Merrilee her belongings and to say good-bye. Merrilee then returned to the room where her adoptive parents were waiting.

The adoptive parents changed Merrilee's name so that she could feel as if she were having a 'fresh start' in her new family. Merrilee had long naturally curly hair. Her foster mother had frequently brushed Merrilee's hair. She did this as a way of being physically close and nurturing with Merrilee. She also used this as a way to raise Merrilee's self esteem by commenting what beautiful hair she had and how pretty she was. The adoptive mother didn't know this history and suggested that Merrilee have her hair cut, 'like your older sister's hair. Merrilee agreed.

I met Merrilee when she was four and a half years old. At that time, she was constantly fighting control battles with her mother. For example, she was not to leave the yard without permission. Merrilee didn't sneak out of the yard; instead, she would sit perched on the fence until she was sure her mother was looking out of the kitchen window. Then, she would go over the fence. If she were asked to do something such as help set the table, it never quite got done.

In some respects she seemed overcompetent, never asking for help. Merrilee had trouble sitting in a comfortable fashion on her parents' laps. She couldn't cuddle. She was prone to many fears, but the most prominent one was her fear of strangers. Whenever the family had company, Merrilee would become alternately hyperactive and clingy, demanding a lot of attention.

**Identifying the needs of the pre-school child and creating an
environment to meet the needs for appropriate autonomy**

**Worksheet**

1. The adoptive parents have contacted you and asked advice about ways
   that they can handle Merrilee's problem behaviour. Using a
   developmental approach, how would you explain Merrilee's behaviour
   to the parents?

2. What recommendations would you make about how to help Merrilee
   exert her autonomy in more appropriate ways?

3. What recommendations would you make with regard to meeting
   Merrilee's dependency needs?

Identifying the needs of the pre-school child and creating an
environment to meet the needs for appropriate autonomy

Sample worksheet

1. The adoptive parents have contacted you and asked advice about ways
   that they can handle Merrilee's problem behaviour. Using a
   developmental approach, how would you explain Merrilee's behaviour
   to the parents?

   *Her behaviour is not 'bad' but an attempt to deal with all
   that has happened to her in the past. Because important
   adults in her life (mother and foster mother) disappeared,
   her sense of trust has been broken and she cannot
   maintain an appropriate balance for her age between
   dependency and autonomy.*

2. What recommendations would you make about how to help Merrilee
   exert her autonomy in more appropriate ways?

   *Find things she can do well and praise her for her
   achievements.*

3. What recommendations would you make with regard to meeting
   Merrilee's dependency needs?

   *The parents need to make her feel loved and valued
   so that it is safe to be dependent. They should do things
   with her eg shopping, outings, having fun together,
   make a 'life story' book. They should promote attachment
   behaviour.*

# Developmental milestones: personal and social

- ## Birth — 1 month

  Looks at face transiently

  Smiles selectively in response to mother's voice at 3 to 4 weeks

  Quiets to human voice at about 3 weeks

  Body tone improves

  Capacity to stay awake grows

  Basic body functions gradually stabilise

- ## 1 — 3 months

  Smiles responsively to human face

  Regards human face

  Tracks human face beyond midline by 8 to 9 weeks

- ## 3 — 6 months

  Orients more toward mother than anyone else

  Uses vocalisation to interact socially

  Probably smiles spontaneously

  Waking periods become longer and better defined

  Individual traits become more obvious

  Attention span increases

  Smiles at image in mirror

  Uses head, eyes, and hands together well in reaching for toy toys and the human face

  May like to play peek-a-boo

  Smiles readily at most people

  Plays alone with contentment

  Takes solid food well

- ## 6 — 9 months

  Begins to be afraid of stranger

  Probably reaches for familiar persons

  Shows desire to be picked up and held

  Feeds self finger foods

  Puts feet in mouth

  Pats mirror image

  Plays peek-a-boo

  Starts drinking from a cup

  Chews and bites on toys at play

  Rarely lies down except when asleep

  Has well established routines

Begins to respond to own name

Begins to respond to 'no, no'

Interacts differently with various family members

May hold own bottle

## • 9 − 12 months

Repeats performances for attention

Acts socially with family; shy with strangers

Begins to develop a sense of identity

Is capable of varying emotions such as fear, anxiety, anger

Begins to develop a sense of humour

Actively seeks attention

Becomes aware of others' emotions

Plays pat-a-cake

May drink from cup by himself

## • 12 − 15 months

Becomes more demanding, assertive, and independent

Has poor emotional equilibrium

Vocalises rather than cries for attention

Has a sense of me and mine

May use spoon, spilling a little

May imitate household tasks

Probably drinks from a cup unassisted

Reacts when mother leaves

## • 15 − 18 months

Claims things as 'mine'

Begins to distinguish 'you' and 'me'

Maintains a concentrated, but wary, interest in strangers

Resists changes in routine or sudden transitions

Expresses autonomy as defiance

Reacts poorly to sharp discipline

Generally is not changed by scolding or verbal persuasion, as words are not yet important enough

Diversion and changing the environment are most useful disciplinary techniques

Does not yet perceive other persons as individuals like himself

Imitates and mimics others

Probably uses spoon well

May help in little household tasks

Probably can take off piece of clothing

Engages in solitary or parallel play

Shows or offers toy to examiner

## • 18 months — 2 years

Continues solitary or parallel play with other children

Is more social with mother

Follows mother

Helps dress and undress self

Washes and dries hands

May indicate wet or soiled nappies

Probably can do simple household tasks

Pulls person to show things

Asks for food and drink

Understands and asks for 'another'

Mimics real life situations during play

Is self-centred but does distinguish between self and others

Conscious of family group

Discriminates edible substances from inedible substances

## • 2 — 3 years

Can put on clothing

Probably can dress self with supervision

Learns to separate from mother easily at about 3 years

Plays interactive games

Is toilet trained

Unzips, zips; unbuckles and buckles; and unbuttons and buttons clothing

Has an identity in terms of name name, sex, and place in family well entrenched by age 2½

Initiates own play activities

Dawdles

Likes praise

Alternates between dependency and self containment

Shows pity, sympathy, modesty, and shame

Has good steering on push toys

Can carry a breakable object

Can pour from one container to another

Often is fearful of certain sounds and noises

Gets drink unassisted

Learns to avoid simple hazards (careful of stairs, stoves, etc)

## • 3 — 4 years

Conforms to the spoken word

Can make 'bargains'

Carries out little errands near home

Is capable of prolonged anxiety or fear

Understands taking turns

Starts to share

Is less rebellious than at 2 or 4

48

Uses language to resist

Toilets self during day

Plays with a group

May dress without supervision by age 4, except for back buttons and tying shoes

Fears loss of parents

Often is fearful of seeing certain objects

Can go on errands in the neighbourhood

Calls attention to own performance

Tends to be bossy and critical of others

Begins to sense time in terms of yesterday, tomorrow, and sense of how long an hour is etc

## • 4 − 5 years

Is dogmatic and dramatic

Argues about parental requests

Control issues prominent for many children

Begins cooperative group play

Has a good imagination

Often has unreasonable fears

May have nightmares

Creates alibis to avoid trouble

Likes silly rhymes, silly sounds, silly names, etc

Is physically aggressive

Probably dresses without assistance, except for back buttons and tying shoes

Washes face and brushes teeth

Is self sufficient in own home

Likes to dress up in grown-up clothes

Laces shoes

# Developmental milestones: fine motor adaptive

- **Birth — 1 month**

  Follows with eyes to midline

  Mouth and eye muscles are the most active muscles

  Has a sucking reflex

  Makes seeking movements with mouth

  Has a grasp reflex, but does not reach

  Hands usually closed

- **1 — 3 months**

  Grasps rattle briefly

  Follows dangling objects past midline

  Puts hands together

- **3 — 6 months**

  Looks at small objects

  May reach for objects frequently using both hands

  Most follow for 180°

  Sucks at hand or fingers

  Regards hands

  Reaches for objects with one hand

May transfer objects from one hand to the other

Looks for objects which leave visual field

Rakes pellet or raisin with hand

Inspects objects with hands, eyes, and mouth

- **6 — 9 months**

  Grasps an object in each hand simultaneously

  Transfers objects from hand to hand

  Probably has a thumb finger grasp

  Develops tongue control

  Begins to develop sense of twoness

  Puts things in and out of container

  Probably works for toy out of reach

- **9 — 12 months**

  Probably has neat pincer grasp

  Bangs together objects held in each hand

  Momentarily brings one object over another

  Grasp release crude

## • 12 — 15 months

Visually prefers circle over other shapes

Has a neat pincer grasp

Puts ball in box

Puts pellet or raisin in bottle

Builds a tower of two cubes

Probably scribbles spontaneously, grasping pen or pencil in the palm

## • 15 — 18 months

Has an exaggerated grasp release

Turns pages several at a time

Knows where things are or belong

Starts to point

Frequently gives evidence of knowing that something has been completed, such as waves "bye-bye" and reports of soiling

Holds spoon

Holds cup

Dumps pellet from bottle after demonstration

May copy vertical line

## • 18 months — 2 years

Builds a tower of four cubes

May build tower of six cubes

Probably imitates a vertical line

Dumps pellet from bottle spontaneously

Strings beads or places rings on spindles

Matches colours frequently

Folds paper once imitatively

Turns pages singly

Can wiggle thumb

Can wiggle tongue

Tries to snip with scissors

Uses colour names incorrectly

Uses number words to accompany serial pointing, a precursor of true counting

Starts to imitate horizontal line

Imitates train with blocks

## • 2 — 3 years

Builds a tower of 8 cubes between 24 and 30 months

Holds pencil by fingers, instead of palmar grasp

Imitates horizontal line well

Draws continuous circles

Can unzip and zip things

Unbuckles after imitation

Adds chimney cube to train

Completes formboard

Likes crayons

Likes puzzle type toys

51

Folds paper lengthwise and crosswise but not diagonal (cannot yet imitate diagonal line with pencil either)

Builds a tower of 9-10 cubes between 30 and 36 months

Probably matches colours, but does not name them correctly

Imitates building of 3 cube bridge

Copies a circle

Buckles after demonstration

Points to simple geometric shapes when named

Completes formboard quickly and correctly

Understands big versus little

Begins to be able to unbutton

Draws a man with 3 parts

May copy a square without demonstration

Probably copies a square after demonstration

Draws unmistakable man, but arms and legs may still come directly from the head

Copies a triangle

Copies linear figures (i e , C, T, L) with rare reversals

May continue to have some problems with diagonals

## • 3 — 4 years

Copies cross

Has a smooth grasp release

Draws picture and names it after drawing

Understands longer versus shorter

Understands 'give me the heavy block'

Draws person with two parts

Can button

Can lace

## • 4 — 5 years

Counts five objects correctly

# Developmental milestones: gross motor

## • Birth — 1 month

Lifts head when on abdomen

Averts head to preferred side when on back; only momentarily to mid-position

Moves extremities equally

## • 1 — 3 months

Lifts head up to $45°$ when on abdomen

Grasps rattle briefly

Holds head erect when held in sitting position

Bears fraction of weight when held in standing position

## • 3 — 6 months

Holds head up to $90°$ when on abdomen

Holds head more frequently at midline

Correlates arm and hand movements in large part with position of head and eyes

Rolls from side to back

Rolls first from abdomen to back

Rolls from back to abdomen

Bears increasing amount of weight when held upright

Head does not lag when pulled to sitting

## • 6 — 9 months

Sits without support

Is increasingly mobile

Stands holding on

Pushes self to sitting

Pulls self to standing at close to 9 months

Leans forward and can push self back to erect position

## • 9 — 12 months

Crawls with left-right alternation

Walks with support

Stands momentarily

Takes a few unsteady steps

## • 12 — 15 months

Stands well alone

Walks well

Stoops and recovers

Falls by collapse

## • 15 — 18 months

Runs stiffly

Climbs up on furniture

Walks backward

Walks into ball in attempt to kick

## • 18 months — 2 years

Kicks ball forward on demonstration

May throw ball over-hand

Walks up steps holding on with one hand, marking time

Gets down stairs on abdomen or bottom

Runs fairly well

Pulls toy as walking

Squats in play

Kicks ball on verbal command by 2 years

## • 2 — 3 years

Jumps in place with both feet

Probably throws ball overhand

Walks on tiptoe after demonstration (many walk on tiptoe spontaneously before)

Tries to pedal tricycle and sometimes succeeds by 2½ years

Tries to stand on one foot

Alternates feet going up stairs

Jumps from bottom step

Probably can pedal tricycle by 3 years

Probably can stand on one foot momentarily by 2½ — 3 years

May do broad jump by 2½ to 3 years

## • 3 — 4 years

Probably can stand on one foot for 5 seconds

May hop on one foot

Probably can do broad jump

## • 4 — 5 years

Probably can hop on one foot

Probably can skip, alternating feet

Probably can catch ball bounced to them

Probably can do forward heel-toe walk

May do backward heel-toe walk

# Language: receptive and expressive

- **Birth — 1 month**

  Cries prior to sleep

  Cries if uncomfortable or in state of tension. Cries are undifferentiated initially but gradually vary with cause

  Responds to bell

  Smiles selectively in response to mother's voice by 3 to 4 weeks

  Quiets to human voice and soft sounds

  Startles to loud sounds

- **1 — 3 months**

  Babbles and coos increasingly

  Most laugh out loud

  Most squeal and gurgle

- **3 — 6 months**

  Crows and squeals

  Spontaneously vocalises vowels consonants, and a few syllables

  Responds to tone of voice and inflection

- **6 — 9 months**

  Says mama and/or dada nonspecifically

Begins to imitate speech sounds

Turns to voice

Many single syllable sounds — ma, da, ba

Spontaneously blows bubbles

- **9 — 12 months**

  Imitates speech sounds

  Obeys 'give it to me'

  Uses 'Dada' and/or 'Mama', specifically as names

  Experiments with sounds

- **12 — 15 months**

  Increases use of jargon

  Communicates by gesture

  Vocalises more than cries for attention

  Usually has 3-5 word vocabulary

  Understands word 'no'

  Shakes head to indicate 'no'

  Points to picture of dog

55

## • 15 — 18 months

Vocalises 'no'

Has a vocabulary of about 10 words

May point to parts of body

Uses words with gestures

Uses jargon fluently

Points to pictures of common objects and may name them as he points

## • 18 months — 2 years

Uses words 'me' and 'mine'

Markedly increases vocabulary

Points consistently to body parts

Combines two to three words

Names pictures of common objects

Follows simple directions

Probably discards jargon during this period

Understands 'your' versus 'my'

Starts to use word 'you'

Uses mostly nouns

## • 2 — 3 years

May use plurals

Say first name

Has a vocabulary of 300 words

Calls self by given name

Uses word 'I' by 2½ years

Speaks with sing-song rhythm

Uses phrases and 3 to 4 word sentences

Probably uses plurals by 2½ to 3 years

May give first and last name by 2½ to 3 years

Uses verbs more often

Begins to use adjectives

Tells own sex by 3 years

By 3 years has a 1,000 word vocabulary

Learns to listen and listens to learn

Asks 'What's that?' often

Probably understands big versus little by 3 years

## • 3 — 4 years

Uses words for ordering perceptions

Uses questions to learn language structure

Probably gives first and last name (not necessarily true for foster children, as last name is rarely stressed at this age for foster children)

Tells age by holding up fingers usually

Probably answers simple comprehensive questions

Probably understands prepositions and starts to use them

Probably understands colour names

Probably understands longer versus shorter

Counts to 3

Repeats 3 to 4 digits

Repeats 3 to 4 nonsense syllables

Has 50 to 75% use of consonants

By age 4, has vocabulary of 1,500 words

## ● 4 — 5 years

Uses colour names

First undertands, then uses adverbs

Uses prepositions

Defines words in terms of use

Understands opposite analogies

Asks lots of why and how questions

Counts out objects correctly to 5 at least; many can count out 8 to 10 objects

Names common coins

Uses consecutive rather than comparative thinking (big, bigger, biggest instead of big versus small)

Loves new words, especially 'funny sounding' words

Tends to talk constantly

Increasing use of imagination

Enjoys humour and self laughing

Probably can identify composition of common objects

Follows 2 to 3 stage command

Can make elaborate replies to questions

Has a vocabulary of 2,000 words or more

Uses all parts of speech correctly

By 5, most infantile articulation disappears

Uses consonants

Corrects own errors in learning to pronounce new words

# The ages six to ten

## The primary task

The primary task for the child between six and ten is to master problems he encounters outside the family unit. The child devotes his energy to learning in school to developing motor skills, and to social interactions primarily with peers of the same sex. The issue of 'fairness' or lack of it in life is important to children at this stage.

## Normal development

### At six

The outstanding characteristic of the six-year-old is poor ability to modulate feelings. The typical six-year-old is very active. He constantly wriggles; bites his nails; kicks tables, or falls off his chair. He is either dancing with delight or drooping in despair.

Sometimes as the child approaches age six, he again aspires to more than he can manage to accomplish easily. He becomes more frequently frustrated; he may scream and have temper tantrums. The six-year-old's insistence on having his own way is a sign that he feels out of control of his life.

The six-year-old is good at starting things, but poor at completing them. He depends on positive direction and guidance from adults. A well-regulated schedule of consistent mealtimes, bedtimes, and other daily rituals is helpful at home. At primary school, he needs a teacher who is in charge in the classroom, but who understands as well the child's need for physical activity and physical closeness.

Not infrequently the six-year-old goes back to sucking his thumb, talking baby talk, and retrieving old favourite stuffed animals from the toy box. The child is usually as confused by this behaviour as parents are. Telling him that he is acting like a baby or making fun of him doesn't help. If parents comment that kids his age often use baby talk, but that they like it better when he talks the way he usually does it will often help. This gives the child a chance to express himself again and the parents a chance to praise him for correct performance.

In general praise works better than discipline with six-year-olds, which means that parents need to look for behaviour they can praise and avoid focusing on negative behaviour. Frequently the creative parent can find behaviour to praise that interferes with undesirable behaviour. Praising a child for putting his hands down works better than reiterating, 'Don't pick your nose!' The focus needs to be on wha the parent wants the child to *do* rather than on what he is *not* to do.

Although the six-year-old enjoys doing tasks *with* someone else, he does not do well when sent off to do a task *for* someone else. 'Let's clean your room together. I'll make your bed while you pick up your clothes and toys', works much better than 'Go and clean your room'. Repeated reminders seem to be necessary for children of this age.

Many six-year-olds take things that belong to others and then lie about their actions. It is not uncommon for a child who has just started school to come home with pockets full of small toys and pencils that he 'found'. Having the child return them to the owner or turn them in to the 'lost and found' is more positive then forcing him to apologise for having taken them.

### At seven

Children calm down as they reach seven. They do not like interruptions and become very absorbed in whatever they are doing. It is not uncommon for a seven-year-old to lie on the floor watching TV or playing before dinner while his mother calls several times for him to come and set the table. The child does not respond, and the mother is convinced that he is 'ignoring' her.

However, he may be concentrating. This is the age at which children learn to screen our distractions and focus on one thing. Children who are not able to do this have serious learning difficulties in school. In fact, it is the inability to focus on one stimulus and screen out others that poses so many problems for the brain-damaged child. If a child seems to have difficulty concentrating, it is a good idea to check and be sure that he isn't suffering from some kind of minimal brain dysfunction. If the parent touches the child who is so busy concentrating that he cannot hear, he will usually startle, but then be able to 'hear' the parent.

Seven-year-olds, like six-year-olds, like physical closeness and occasional quick touching from the teacher. Children at seven still depend on reminders and guidance from adults. When they're upset, they become sullen and withdrawn. It's at this age that children frequently stamp off and slam doors. Seven-year-olds need reassurance from adults that it is okay to make mistakes, and they need help correcting those mistakes. They don't respond well to lectures or scoldings.

Many children in the first or second classes at school have high expectations of themselves. Such a child may be frequently disappointed and frustrated by his own performances. The child may act out or start crying, feel embarrassed, and then feel even more frustrated. If this sequence of events occurs at school, the child may still have a lot of uncomfortable feelings when he returns home. It is quite common in these circumstances for the child to pick a fight with a parent so that he can release his pent-up feelings. This doesn't mean the child plans this kind of event; it just happens because he is not yet very good at handling strong feelings.

Adults often wish children would just talk about their feelings.

59

However, children of this age still have difficulties talking instead of acting out when they feel things strongly. They may be able to talk about the feelings in retrospect. The goal of the supportive parent in this situation is to help the child learn more appropriate ways of expressing frustration while, at the same time, not making the child feel that he is 'wrong' or 'bad'.

The seven-year-old has not learned to lose. Frequently if a child this age sees that he is going to lose, the game never quite gets finished. The playing board gets upset, or the child provokes the parent to say, 'If the game isn't going to be fun, just put it away'. Children of this age still frequently cheat in order to win. They have little sense of humour and cannot be handled with humour. They tend to think that people are laughing *at* them. They are becoming aware of 'fairness' and 'luck' and a frequent comment from seven on, for several years, is 'It's not fair'.

Reasoning can be used with the child who constantly bombards the parent with cries of 'It's not fair!' One such approach is to say to the child, 'Now let me get this straight. You want me to treat you just the same as your brother?' The child usually agrees. 'So the next time Johnny needs a spanking, you want a spanking too?' 'Well, I don't know about that'. About that time fairness seems to lose its powers — at least for the moment.

Of course, true fairness in dealing with children is not always equalising everything, but rather giving to each according to his needs. Some children need more attention than others; some need more discipline than others. In fact equalising everything for siblings poses many more problems than it solves. It implies that the child is in no way special or unique and that, in and of itself, does irreparable harm to the child's self esteem.

Most seven-year-olds can tell time and can recite the months of the year, although it is common that in such a recitation they may accidently omit one or two months. They have an understanding of the order in which seasons occur. Their internal sense of time is also emerging.

## At eight

Eight is an expansive age. The eight-year-old tends to be selfish at times and demand considerable attention; at other times he is gay and cheerful. The eight-year-old is impatient with himself and with others. He may be pert in his talk with family members. He is very curious about what others are doing so he may seem nosey as well. Verbally he is often out of bounds. He boasts, exaggerates, and may share private family information with virtual strangers.

The eight-year-old is improving his gross muscle skills, but accidents are common as he misjudges what he can do. He is just beginning to be capable of sustained group activity and is learning to lose at games. He is very sensitive about receiving criticism, especially in front of others.

He is also interested in his past history; the eight-year-old loves to drag out the baby books and family albums, and loves to hear about his own escapades as a younger child. He also is very interested in the future and what it will hold for him. He may be sure that he will become an Olympic medallist or a movie star. It is best that parents treat these boasts as possible long-range goals. Time will put the child's true potential into perspective — who knows, this child may be a future gold medallist!

Eight-year-olds express a deepening interest in life and life processes. They are better observers than they were at seven. They begin to see conclusions, contexts, and implications that they didn't see before.

Eight-year-olds begin to have a sense of humour. Eight is the age of the riddle. Nothing infuriates an eight more than having his riddle ruined when his sibling pops up with the answer.

## At nine

Although the typical nine-year-old does experience quick extreme emotional shifts, they are short-lived and thus he appears to be more stable. The child of this age is becoming more independent. He is more responsible, cooperative, and dependable. He is capable of concentrating for several hours. This is the optimum age for the child to perfect his proficiency in basic subjects at school. In fact, if the child cannot read, use basic maths concepts, and write by now, it is unlikely that he will acquire these skills without considerable special effort on the part of both the child and the school.

Nine-year-olds like to plan ahead. They may appear absent-minded, but they are usually just busy thinking. They like to classify, identify, and order information. Frequently nine-year-olds take up a collecting type hobby.

The nine-year-old is beginning to learn to function within a group and to subordinate his own interests to those of the group. In fact, at school the teacher becomes more of a facilitator, and peer pressures becomes increasingly important.

Nine-year-olds work hard and play hard. They become interested in competitive sports and although they may not like to lose, they learn to lose. In fact, a nine-year-old's interest in sports is primarily related to the social aspects of the game — an attitude that frustrates more competitive parents.

## At ten

Age ten, like age five, is a nodal stage when the child's perceptions and abilities seem to coincide. Ten-year-olds seem relaxed and casual. They can participate in discussions of social and world problems. In fact, it is a good time for parents to share their values on these matters with their children.

Friends are coming into direct competition with the family for the ten-year-old's time and for his esteem. It is not uncommon for a ten-year-old to believe something a friend has said over something the parent has said. Boys may fight and wrestle and shove and punch to show friendship, while girls hold hands, gossip, and write notes to one another. Sharing secrets and pondering mysteries with friends delight children of this age.

61

Ten-year-olds enjoy family activities as long as they don't interfere with activities with friends. Peer influence is important so ten-year-ol do not like to be singled out in front of friends. A wise parent or teacher knows it is more effective at this age to criticise, correct, and praise the child in private rather than in front of a class or even other family members.

## Minimising the trauma of separation

### Ages 6-10

Because the child this age usually has reasonably good verbal skills an has developed some internalised sense of time, the preparation proces for forthcoming moves is accomplished more easily than in the pre-school age child. However, adults need still to be listening for signs of magical thinking or misperceptions. The clues and cues to these usually are easier to identify in the child this age than in the younger child.

Adequate pre-placement preparation can go a long way in helping children of these ages understand forthcoming moves and resolve feelings about them. When pre-placement preparation is impossible because of an emergency move, we still can help the child understand what has happened in retrospect.

A major focus in helping the child deal with moves is to help him identify his underlying feelings and deal with them. A second major focus for children this age should be on their being an active part of t moving process. Although the child needs reassurance that the adults are ultimately responsible for the decision making about the move, they need to know that we can only do our job well if they share with us their feelings — worries, concerns, hopes, and dreams — about the move.

## Children ages six to ten in placement

Those who work with children of this age group in placement need to be particularly keyed to two development issues. The first of these is the normal development of assertion and anger. This is critical because angry or assertive responses by children in placement may be normal, but very often set off serious repercussions such as another move or severing of a relationship.

The second key issue is the effects of separation and loss on development at this stage. These two issues are discussed in the remainder of this section.

### Assertion and anger

Between five and a half and six, as the child enters the period of emotional disequilibrium, aggressiveness tends to return. Since the youngster is going through an age of increasing frustration, there tends to be a recurrence of temper tantrums. This is an ideal time to teach a child more appropriate ways to express frustration since the child has verbal and intellectual skills he did not previously possess. The child may destroy things if sent to his room or he may refuse to remain in the room because of his increased aggressiveness. He is quite likely to call people names; these names are most likely to be bathroom words such as 'you are a big piece of poop'. He is also likely to make verbal threats. Overall, he tends to contradict, argue, and resist. He may hit or kick at adults who confront him and may hit or kick at other children. Cruelty towards animals may also be present at this age.

Seven-years-olds are less aggressive and have fewer tantrums. They exhibit less resistance to requests. The most common objection children make at this age is 'It isn't fair.' If angry, the seven-year-old may stalk off to his room by himself; in general he prefers to withdraw from his parents rather than stay and fight as he did at six.

The typical eight-year-old shows even less aggression overall. He responds to attack or criticism with hurt feelings, rather than aggression. When he's very angry, he may become aggressive verbally. Name calling may still be present.

By age nine the swearing shifts from a vocabulary related to elimination to a vocabulary with sexual words. Fighting and 'beating him up' are common talk among boys, but again the actual aggression is more likely to be verbal than physical. Nine is critical of others and may object to what others say or do.

It is not uncommon for a child of ten to have one last physical tantrum when confronted by parents about something. It is as though the child is asking 'Can you still control me?' Following such an outburst the child is quite likely to be very embarrassed by his own behaviour. However, ten with his overall emotional equilibrium is not characteristically an angry age. Crying is a common response to anger at this age.

Reactions to separations or losses between age six and ten
Again, child placement workers need to be particularly aware of the effects of separation and losses that occur as a child passes through the stages of development described here. Separations or losses during these years are less likely to be contaminated by magical thinking or misperceptions than are separations at earlier ages. However, even with the child's increased ability to understand and conceptualise, he cannot handle separations or losses without supportive help.

Helping a child understand that he may have more than one feeling about a loss or separation, and that having mixed feelings is normal can help. For example, a child of this age can identify that 'part of me feels sad and part of me feels mad.' However, because of the emphasis on fairness at this age, the child may get caught spending all of his energy on 'why me' or 'it's not fair' and not move further in terms of resolution of the loss.

The child's ability to understand time is important in terms of adjustment to shorter separations. However, the child's fear of the unknown means that we must be as honest as possible with him about what is happening now, what we think will happen in the future, and when events will occur.

If the child of this age is spending his emotional energy coping with his feelings about separations and losses, this may interfere with his ability to accomplish the primary developmental tasks of this age, including learning in school and developing friendships with other children of the same sex. Separations and losses during these ages may cause a temporary regression to earlier stages of thinking (ie a reversion to magical thinking) or less mature behaviour. They may also interrupt the normal progression of conscience development.

Another important aspect of development to keep in mind in terms of children in care is the need for the child during the latency years to learn more about himself as a baby and pre-school child and to incorporate this knowledge into his continually emerging self identity. Children in care who do not have access to information about their early years and about their birth parents have difficulty in terms of self identity issues.

It is important that parents who adopt children at younger ages be aware that their children will need to know more about their past as they reach the latency ages. Adoptive parents must understand that this need in no way reflects upon the child's attachment to the adoptive family, but rather relates to a healthy desire to increase knowledge about themselves and integrate it into their self identity.

Increasingly, social workers, foster parents, and adoptive parents are being asked to deal with latency age children who have been sexually abused in previous homes. These children, by a variety of behaviours, indicate underlying developmental needs. They particularly need parenting which clarifies for them alternate modes of parent-child interactions and allows them to experience physically nurturing non-sexual relationships.

64

*Exercise 5:*
Dealing with a sexually abused child using a developmental approach

Instructions

*Purpose:*

To help you learn to deal with a sexually abused child using a
developmental approach.

*How to do it:*

1. Read Rhonda's case history.

2. Answer the questions on the worksheet for Exercise 5. Then, compare
   your own answers with those of another caseworker on the sample
   worksheet.

### Rhonda's case

*Rhonda is seven years old. Her mother died two years ago after a long
illness during which she was repeatedly hospitalised. Prior to her death,
Rhonda's mother had told her own mother (Rhonda's grandmother)
that she thought that her husband had been sexually abusing Rhonda.
She said she had confronted him and he had denied abusing Rhonda.
Rhonda's mother was concerned about what would happen after she
died and told her mother that she had told Rhonda to tell her grandmother if Daddy did anything 'naughty' to her.*

*Following her mother's death, Rhonda took over the mothering of
her younger brother. The babysitter noticed this both before and after
school when she had both children while Rhonda's dad worked. The
babysitter also commented that when the father came to pick up the
children after work, Rhonda would run and kiss him on the lips. She'd
greet him with a comment such as 'Did you have a hard day at work,
Daddy?'*

*Her teacher had noted that Rhonda was 'daydreaming constantly'
and falling behind in school. She has few friends and isolates herself
during playtime. Recently the grandmother made an unannounced
visit to the home and found Rhonda's father lying on top of her with
both his and her clothes partially off. The grandmother contacted the
welfare agency. Rhonda and her brother were removed from the home
and taken into care. Rhonda's father is awaiting trial on charges of
sexual abuse.*

Worksheet

1. From a developmental standpoint what are the issues involving Rhonda with regard to sexual development and sexual identification?

2. What behaviours might one expect to see in Rhonda in placement?

3. Knowing that Rhonda experienced the loss of her mother during the Oedipal stage and the stage of magical thinking, how do you think Rhonda perceived and coped with the loss of the mother?

*Exercise 5:*

**Dealing with a sexually abused child using a developmental approach**

Worksheet

4. What would you expect Rhonda's reaction to separation from the
   father to be? How might she perceive this reaction?

5. What type of foster home would you select for Rhonda?

6. How would you advise the foster parents in terms of meeting Rhonda's
   needs with regard to developmental issues in the area of sexual
   identification?

*Exercise 5:*

**Dealing with a sexually abused child using a developmental approach**

**Sample worksheet**

1. From a developmental standpoint what are the issues involving Rhonda with regard to sexual development and sexual identification?

   She lost her mother during the oedipal stage when she needed to feel that her mother was not upset by her feelings for her father. She needed to be able to identify with her mother to resolve this stage.

2. What behaviours might one expect to see in Rhonda in placement?

   She may be very sexually provocative with men. She may daydream a lot and not concentrate. She may have a lot of fears, nightmares etc. She may find it difficult to relate to a foster mother.

3. Knowing that Rhonda experienced the loss of her mother during the Oedipal stage and the stage of magical thinking, how do you think Rhonda perceived and coped with the loss of the mother?

   She will blame herself and feel her 'magical thoughts' have come true. She will feel herself to be omnipotent and yet be frightened and guilty. She coped by trying to take her mother's place with the father and being a mother to her younger brother.

*Exercise 5:*

**Dealing with a sexually abused child using a developmental approach**

Sample worksheet

---

4. What would you expect Rhonda's reaction to separation from the father to be? How might she perceive this reaction?

*Both relief and a sense of loss. She will feel she is being punished, deservedly, for her 'bad thoughts' about her mother.*

---

5. What type of foster home would you select for Rhonda?

*Foster parents who are comfortable with sexual issues and with each other.*

---

6. How would you advise the foster parents in terms of meeting Rhonda's needs with regard to developmental issues in the area of sexual identification?

*They need to help Rhonda identify with a woman and accept her femininity, and to feel valued in a non-sexual relationship with a man. They need to be alert to correct her magical thinking.*

# Section 5 Adolescence

## The overall task

Although many people equate adolescence with the teenage years, the physical and emotional changes that mark adolescence start at age 11 This is especially true for girls who, on the whole, tend to mature physically two years ahead of boys. In this section, we will discuss ages 11 to 16 as the adolescent years. The chart below highlights the sequence of physical changes that mark adolescence.

## Sequence of physical changes
*Figure 1*

*Female*
1. breast enlargement
2. development of straight pubic hair
3. maximum growth spurt
4. development of kinky pubic hair
5. onset of menstruation
6. development of axillary hair

*Male*
1. growth in size of testes
2. straight pubic hair
3. increased size of penis
4. beginnings of voice changes
5. first ejaculation
6. maximum growth spurt
7. axillary hair
8. marked voice change
9. development of beard

From Normal Adolescence: Group for Advancement of Psychiatry New York, 1968

## Normal development

Adolescents are moody. Normally they alternate between being unreliable and being dependable and responsible. As they separate from the family, they are likely to oppose family rules, values, and expectations. They seem to be preoccupied with complying with the peer group and opposing the family. At the same time they have a strong need to belong in the family and to be taken seriously.

Adolescents have both abundant sexual and aggressive impulses. It i important that adults help them separate these two issues and learn to deal with each in socially acceptable ways.

The psychological tasks to be accomplished in adolescence bear a marked similarity to those of the pre-school years. The task of the pre-school child is to separate from family members, particularly his mother, and to become an independent individual within the family structure. During adolescence, an individual must find his place in the world at large just as during the pre-school years he needed to clarify his place within the family. To do this the child frequently acts in opposition to the family as a whole.

Adolescence is an age when control battles between parent and child emerge again and when frustration is a prominent part of the child's experience. Any issues that were poorly handled during the pre-school years may re-emerge during the adolescent years. Adolescence provides an opportunity for re-cycling and successfully solving unresolved developmental issues.

In general, during adolescence, young people experience a year of opening horizons with new difficulties followed by a year of consolidation of gains. In other words, both parents and children can expect a year filled with crises to be followed by a year with some measure of reprieve in which to repair relationships and enjoy each other before the next stage is reached.

## At eleven

The typical eleven-year-old shows some similarities both the early toddler stage and to the child of five and half to six. He is again emotionally unstable, and he is always in motion. He is assertive, curious, investigative, talkative, and sociable. He has a vast appetite both for food and for experience. He can fly into rage at short notice and burst out laughting with little provocation. He tires easily. He is in such a state of disequilibrium that even his temperature control is uneven; he always seems to be either too hot or too cold.

The child of this age is starting to see parents as individuals, not just as parents and is becoming critical of them. Frequently, adjusting at school comes easier than adjusting at home. In general his best behaviour is away from home.

At this age children hate to go to bed at night and hate to get up in the morning. Although they usually begin to take an interest in clothes, they usually don't take good care of them. Eleven-year-olds hate work and frequently spend more energy avoiding tasks than it would take to accomplish them.

This is the poorest age for getting along with siblings. The eleven-year-old likes school more for friends than for learning. He competes for grades and in athletics. Eleven and 12 are the most fearful of the adolescent years. Fear of wild animals, snakes, bugs, and ghosts is common.

## At twelve

The typical twelve-year-old is less insistent, more reasonable, and more companionable. He tries to win the approval of others. Although his peer group is increasingly important to him, he is less competitive within it than he was at eleven. He is able to do more independent work at school and, in general, needs less supervision. In fact school, at this age, is a source of great satisfaction for most children because of their

71

capacity for prolonged periods of factual learning and because of the increase in conceptual ability. If the child has problems in school, the one of his major chances for positive feedback is eliminated. Twelve enjoys discussions and debates, but he is calmer in his arguments than he was at eleven and doesn't resist just for the sake of doing so.

This is normally a period that favours integration of the personalit Parents often describe twelve-year-olds as likeable. The child of this age has a great enthusiasm for things he likes and hatred for the he dislikes. He is able to deal with others, and can be dealt with, through humour.

There is a wide range of difference noted in the rate of physical growth among twelve-year-old boys. Twelves show an increasing interest in the opposite sex. Yet because of the wide difference in the rate of development between girls and boys there are resulting variations in their interest in the opposite sex.

### At thirteen

Age thirteen shows a certain resemblance to seven. Compared to the twelve-year-old, he is less outgoing and inquisitive and may sometimes seem withdrawn and moody. He uses his withdrawal from the family as a chance to mull over and incorporate experiences; the withdrawal is not an indication of retreat from reality. Thirteen-year-olds are reflective. They spend a lot of time in front of the mirror, as well as reflecting mentally. This is an age when most adolescents are going through marked physical changes and much of the time in front of mirrors is spent integrating the 'new' person with the old self-perceptions. The mirror fosters self discovery and self assurance.

The thirteen-year-old is very sensitive to criticism. He may be critical of his parents, but usually this criticism concerns problems that he is trying to resolve himself. This is a good age for parents to back off, because of the thirteen's sensitivity to criticism.

Thirteen-year-olds are more likely to be annoyed or irritated than to have outbursts of anger. They are not as demonstrative. At the same time they are more aware of their own feelings.

Again, for good students, school is a source of satisfaction. The child of this age is better able to organise his time in school; his concentration is more sustained and his self control is more evident. He becomes selective about what he chooses to compete in and usually chooses things he is good at.

### At fourteen

At fourteen children typically become expansive and outgoing again. They are less withdrawn and seem happier. They seem to enjoy life. They are friendly both at home and away. Although they may be highly embarrassed by parental conduct, the relationships within the family are less tense. The fourteen-year-old and his family have more respect for each other and confidence in each other. Fourteen-year-olds seem to be more objective and capable of self appraisal than they were at thirteen. They will look at both sides of an issue.

Girls at age fourteen usually have the bodies of young women, while many boys have not yet matured physically. This is an age when further sex education is both needed and eagerly received. This is the peak age for telephone calls for girls. Since many of the girls phone boy boys, it may be a peak age for incoming calls for boys as well. The telephone not only allows the adolescent to spend more time with peers without ever leaving home, but it also allows the adolescent to talk about sex and relate to members of the opposite sex without risk of it leading to immediate sexual encounters.

### At fifteen

Fifteen-year-olds are frequently lazy or indifferent — they don't appear to expend much energy. In reality their energies are focused inwardly rather than outwardly. Although most children are not as intensely moody as they were at thirteen, there is a similarity in the way they withdraw from the family. This, as at thirteen, is related to pre-occupation with feelings.

Fifteen-year-olds are experiencing a growing self awareness and perceptiveness, though they tend to cover up their feelings in front of others. They are trying to sort out their own potential and limitations. They seem to resist even reasonable restrictions imposed by others as a way of asserting independence.

### At sixteen

Sixteen-year-olds seem self assured and self reliant. By now both the adolescent and his parents take his increased independence for granted. In general, there are fewer arguments between parents and adolescent. Sixteen-year-olds have their emotions pretty well in hand and seem to be not so touchy or moody.

## Minimising the trauma of separation

### In adolescence

The adolescent is usually a very active participant in the moving process, both prior to the move, during the move, and during the post-placement period. The adjustment is likely to be smoother if the adolescent feels that his thoughts and desires are being fully considered in the moving process.

Contracting and getting firm verbal and/or written commitments from the adolescent about how he is willing to work at making the placement succeed are techniques that increase the likelihood of successful placements.

Because major issues for adolescence revolve around separation — individuation, control issues, and sexual issues — these should be addressed directly during the placement process. If the adolescent thinks that adults are trying to make all decisions for him or are trying to control him, he is likely to rebel more in a behavioural manner. If he thinks that he has been part of the entire decision-making process, such rebellion is both less likely and more easily confronted if it does occur. Statements such as, 'I'm confused; before moving you said that you thought the rules in this group home were reasonable; now you seem to be bent on breaking them' can be used if rebellion does occur. This opens the door for the adolescent both to talk about how he feels and to take responsibility for his own behaviour.

## Adolescents in placement

In this section, the information that is highlighted has special relevance to work with adolescents in placement. First, normal assertion and anger during adolescence is discussed. Again, this aspect of development is highlighted because normal expression of assertion and anger by adolescents in placement is much too often misconstrued and perhaps the cause of over-reaction. Understanding normal development can help sort out a particular adolescent's behaviour. In addition, this section highlights the effects of separation and loss on children in adolescence and some of the problems posed by trying to integrate the adolescent into a new family.

### Assertion and anger in adolescence

It is important to remember that control issues emerge again in adolescence because the child is again working on making a psychological separation from the family. Children at age eleven get angry more often than they did at ten. It is common for children this age to yell, hit, and slam doors. Rather violent verbal retorts are common. It is the poorest age for getting along with younger siblings.

Twelve-year-olds may still strike out physically or throw things when they are angry. However, this is the last age at which an immediate physical response to anger is usually seen. Verbal responses become more and more frequent. Twelve-year-olds often assert themselves by 'talking back' to parents. At thirteen, the most common response to anger is leaving the room. Sulking is common and there may be tears in the eyes in response to anger.

Fourteen-year-olds do not anger especially easily. Physical responses and crying are much less common than they were previously. Swearing, name calling, and sarcasm are sometimes used; however, even more important aspect of this is raised by the adolescent who has lost parental figures earlier in life and who do not have sufficient memories for the separation and identification process. It is common for adolescents to need further information about their birth parents at this time and to come to further resolution about the separation and loss of these parental figures if the psychological tasks of adolescence are to be accomplished. Adolescents in placement, whether it be foster or adoptive placement, use both the parental figures with whom they are living and the memories or information about the birth parents during their struggle for independence.

Placing an adolescent into a new home poses special problems, particularly if it is an adoptive home. It is difficult to encourage attachment and bonding between parent and child when the primary developmental task is for the adolescent to find his place in the world, separate from other family members. Such placement may work best if the adolescent makes a firm commitment to the new relationship and if the new parents understand the difficulties they may face in building bonds with a child at this age. The parents must be firmly committed to helping the adolescent achieve a balance between attachment and independence. Because the oppositional drives seem strongest in early adolescence adoptive placements undertaken between the ages of 12-14 seem to face more difficulties than those undertaken later in adolescence at ages 15-16 (Jewett, 1980).

When adolescents are placed in foster homes or in adoptive homes, parental figures must be cognisant of the adolescent sexual issues, so that they can be supportive in helping the child resolve such issues at the same time as they form non-sexual relationships with the adolescent.

With the increasing incidence of sexual abuse, even in the young child, all social workers and alternative parents must learn to become more comfortable dealing with the sexual issues which are emerging in such a large proportion of cases in child care.

Exercise 6 that follows deals with identifying unmet developmental needs in the older child.

*Exercise 6:*

Identifying unmet needs in the older child and creating an
environment to meet these needs

**Instructions**

*Purpose:*

To help you learn to identify unmet development needs in the older
child and to plan to meet those needs.

*How to do it:*

1. Read Tracy's case history.

2. Answer the questions on the worksheet for Exercise 6. Then, compare
   your own answers with those of another caseworker on the sample
   worksheet.

### Tracy's case

*Tracy is 12. She was recently placed for adoption. Her birth family had a wide variety of problems. Her father is an alcoholic and frequently was gone from home for extended periods of time. Her mother had periods of depression. She was sexually promiscuous between her depressive episodes. Although Tracy had been visually exposed to many adult sexual encounters, there was no history of direct sexual abuse. There had, however, been some episodes of physical abuse by both the birth mother and the mother's various boyfriends.*

*Following one episode of physical abuse when she was eight, Tracy was placed in care. Attempts at intervention in terms of helping the family to be better able to meet Tracy's needs were unsuccessful because her birth parents did not follow through on any of the recommendations. Their parental rights were terminated when Tracy was 11.*

*In her adoptive home Tracy is the middle of three children; the other two are boys. The adoptive parents complain that Tracy is always underfoot and never gives them a moment of privacy. She constantly hangs to one or the other of them. She even 'hangs' on to the boys. She constantly interrupts adult conversations. When her parents' friends come to visit, she hangs onto them and asks very personal questions that show no sign of tact.*

*When Tracy doesn't get her own way, she tends to pout, whine, and may retreat, crying to her room. Although she likes to help her adoptive mother, her mother gets tired of having her underfoot. Frequently she asks Tracy to clean up her room or to dust in another part of the house. Such requests are usually met with passive non-compliance. Tracy will go to her room, but she will not complete the job.*

*Tracy does not do very well in terms of self-care skills. She takes baths or showers only when reminded. Frequently she comes to the table with dirty hands and face and unkempt hair unless specifically reminded to clean up for dinner. She hates to wash her hair. She likes her mother to wash her hair and is especially pleased if her mother curls her hair.*

*At school Tracy is behind academically. In spite of receiving extra help she gets poor marks. The teacher complains that she is very immature, that the other girls her age call her 'baby' and avoid her. Tracy is prone to nightmares. She is afraid of the dark and is afraid of thunder at night.*

**Identifying unmet needs in the older child and creating an environme**
**to meet these needs**

## Worksheet

1. At what overall developmental level does Tracy seem to be functioning?

2. What advice would you give to her adoptive parents about the following behaviours:

— her hanging on behaviours:

— her constant interrupting:

— her whining and pouting:

— her poor self-help skills:

— her desire to help but refusal to do a good job when left on her own:

— her fears:

*Exercise 6:*

**Identifying unmet needs in the older child and creating an environment to meet these needs**

Sample Worksheet

---

1. At what overall developmental level does Tracy seem to be functioning?

   Somewhere between a toddler and a five to six year old.

---

2. What advice would you give to her adoptive parents about the following behaviours:

   Overall to help them understand the level she is functioning at and the need to achieve a balance between attachment and independence.

---

— her hanging on behaviours:

   Be patient. Find ways of encouraging attachment and positive interaction.

---

— her constant interrupting:

   Ask her to wait her turn but give her lots of opportunities for conversation.

---

— her whining and pouting:

   Praise her if she can deal positively with a situation — look for positive ways out of situations rather than battles she has to lose.

---

— her poor self-help skills:

   Help her to get into a routine by patient reminders, praise, for remembering and looking nice, and doing the things she likes eg curling her hair.

---

— her desire to help but refusal to do a good job when left on her own:

   Do things with her at first and praise her for her achievements.

---

— her fears:

   Establishing comfortable bed time rituals eg talking, reading, playing a game together. Leave a night light.

---

# Special developmental issues

In this final section we highlight four special developmental issues: fears and worries, temper tantrums, conscience development, and sexual issues. These issues were selected because of their particular relevance to children in placement. Some of these issues, such as temper tantrums, are likely to be of particular concern to the biological, foster, and adoptive parents involved in a particular child. Others, like fears and worries, are included because they are often problematic for the child in placement and those problems need to be detected.

## Fears and worries

There are common, normal fears and worries that accompany each stage of child development. The parents' job is to help the child cope with and overcome these fears. Parents should *not* belittle the child or make him feel inadequate because of his fears — this cannot possibly help the child learn to feel brave and capable. Nor must they reassure the child excessively or try to remove all possibilities for fear as this is an impossible task.

The child has enough fears to cope with so that parental figures should not add to the fears by use of threats. A child's fears of abandonment are exacerbated by threats of leaving him if he has a temper tantrum in the grocery store. A child who has a fear of going to the doctor is not helped by a threat of 'If you don't stop crying, I will tell the doctor to give you an injection.' If a child is going through a stage of many fears with regard to strange noises, the parents should not make loud, scary sounds to teach the child to get over the fear.

Acknowledging that the child is afraid while providing some comfort, will give the child more strength to overcome the fear. The parent may ask the verbal child if there is any way that the parent can help him with the fear.

During the first year of life infants usually startle in response to fear producing sensation. Loud or unexpected noises are frequently frightening to the infant. Sudden movements may stimulate fear in him. Threats of falling, or being dropped, as well as threats of bodily harm or pain lead to fear reactions.

During the first half of the second year, the child becomes afraid of separations from his mother and may cry vigorously when he sees her leave. The sounds of mechanical gadgets, particularly those that move, such as vacuum cleaners and certain mechanical toys, provoke fear

80

during this period.

The two-year-old is afraid of noises such as trains, thunder, animal sounds, or flushing toilets. The two-year-old may have fears of going down the drain. Separation from mother, particularly at bedtime, may still scare the two-year-old.

During the second half of the second year the child is also prone to spatial fears. He may fear being moved rapidly himself, and he may also react to having objects in his environment moved from their usual place. He notices and objects to being taken by a different car route to a known place. He is fearful of large objects approaching him.

Visual fears predominate in three-year-old. The child at this age is frequently fearful of masks, costumes, strange appearing objects, the dark, and animals. The fear of being left alone at night is still present, and the three-year-old may react adversely to separation from the parents at nighttime while accepting daytime separations with a measure of grace.

Since the child's imagination emerges between the ages of three and a half and four, he becomes prone to fearful thoughts and to fearful dreams. The four-year-old is fearful of a wide variety of stimuli. Sirens and other loud sharp noises provoke fear. It is not uncommon for the four-year-old to be frightened of people who look 'different.' This may include people with physical disabilities, the elderly, or people of a different race from those he is accustomed to seeing. A fear of animals is frequently still present and many four-year-olds are very afraid of bugs. Fear of the dark is the single most common fear of the four-year-old. The child may want a night light or may want the parent to precede him into the room at bedtime before the light is turned on. If the parent agrees to such simple measures, it will help the child learn to trust that he has good ideas about how to overcome his own fears.

Sometimes children are afraid that something may be hiding under the bed. If the child wishes to look under the bed while the parent is there, that is fine. However, if the parent joins in the search for hidden fearful objects, this may imply that the parent, too, believes that something might be present.

The child this age uses the word 'afraid' or 'scared' and may even enjoy being mildly frightened by an adult in play if, in general, adults in his life have been trustworthy. Since the four-year-old is able to imagine things, he is commonly fearful of 'monsters,' or 'bogeymen.' This fear is frequently associated with his fear of the dark. Overall, his fears seem unreasonable to the adults in his life.

One of the pre-school child's greatest fears is that his parents will not be available when he needs them. Threats of separation of abandonment should *never* be used with the pre-school age child.

A common fear seen in children in foster care is fear of the water. This may be very extreme and may relate to any form of bathing or swimming, particularly if it involves getting the face and head wet. Frequently adults assume that the child has been threatened with drowning or has been held under water. Although this has happened in some rare child care cases, most of the time this extreme fear is not

81

based on real events. It more likely relates to an overall lack of trust that others will not protect the child and keep him safe.

In general, five is not a particularly fearful age until the child reaches the disequilibrium that usually occurs between ages five and half and six. Most of the fears of the early five-year-old are concrete down-to-earth fears, such as fear of bodily harm, fear of falling, or fear of being bitten by a dog. Thunder or sirens at night might be fear-arousing. The fear that mother will not be available when needed is still present and demonstrates itself in terms of fears that mother will be lost or will not be home when the child returns from school.

It is common for a six-year-old to be afraid of thunder, lightning, and fire. Six also has a fear of deformities and a fear that mother may die. He is very fearful of even slight injuries to himself, and he responds out of all proportion to the extent of the injury. Every parent has had the experience of hearing their six-year-old scream that he is bleeding. The parent goes running, expecting that a trip to the hospital for stitches is imminent, and finds the child immobilised by a small scratch on the finger. Rather than ridicule the child or minimise his fears, it is best to wash it, bandaid it, give the child an extra squeeze, and reassure him that it will heal quickly because he has a fine healthy body. This fear seems related to the child's emerging awareness combined with his lack of awareness of what the long-term effects of his own minor injuries may be.

Seven-year-olds fear the unknown and are quite likely to be fearful when they find themselves in a new or unfamiliar situation. However, they are beginning to learn ways to cope with their own fears, and they are no longer so dependent upon adults to help with them. Frequently they are ashamed of fears and may be embarrassed if they are seen crying.

By age eight, the child's fears are decreasing although they may fear not being liked. Eight-year-olds love to frighten others with snakes and bugs and scary stories.

Nine-year-olds do not have as many fears, but they have worries. They are upset by their own mistakes and worried about school failure. They enjoy frightening others and being frightened themselves. They are, in fact, proud of being 'frightened to death', but living through it. Nine-year-olds are not afraid if mother is not home after school so long as they know what to expect.

Ten overall is a less fearful age than the next two years. Fears of being killed or kidnapped may be present.

Eleven and twelve are the most fearful of the adolescent years. Children of these ages tend to worry about things they fear. Wild animals, snakes, and being alone in the dark are common fears. The fear of the dark is frequently related to lights shining in from outside a house causing shadows. Sounds that are not understood at night lead to fears of intruders. Twelve has similar fears. Worries usually centre on school and social concerns.

During the remaining adolescent years, fears become less prominent. Worries about personal appearance, social acceptance, popularity, grades, performing in public, applying for a job, and their personal future increase during adolescence as fears decrease. Some adolescents even worry about not worrying enough.

## Temper tantrums

Understanding the causes of temper tantrums makes their occurrence more predictable. Ways to manage them also become apparent. Temper tantrums occur when three conditions are present simultaneously:

1. The child has a great need or desire.
2. He has an inability to achieve this need or desire.
3. He does not know how to express the frustration in an appropriate way.

Temper tantrums are most common between the ages of one and three. The child has a great need during this time to become independent and to feel 'big', yet he frequently fails to achieve this. He runs into opposition from others, and he faces his own physical limitations. It is not realistic to expect the toddler to be able to express his frustrations 'appropriately' by adult standards. Of course, children differ in their ability to tolerate frustration and thus in their propensity to temper tantrums.

During the toddler years, some children do best if they are ignored during the tantrum, while others need to be physically close to an adult If the child becomes so out of control that he starts to hurt himself or others, then the parent should physically control him. Allowing children to feel out of control is very threatening to them. They recognise they cannot stop their own behaviour and if no one else will stop them, they are at the mercy of all their internal impulses.

At any rate, during a temper tantrum, the child is uncomfortable. When the temper tantrum is over and the discomfort alleviated, he is very open to nurturance and acceptance by an adult. At the *end* of the temper tantrum, it is possible to build attachment between a child and an adult. This is when a child needs reassurance that the adult understands that he was frustrated, not 'bad', and that he is still loved. For the toddler all this can be communicated by physical comforting and closeness.

The four-year-old frequently has a recurrence of temper tantrums with his increased stubbornness and resistance. The child between five and a half and six whose abilities have not yet caught up with his perceptions is again prone to temper tantrums. This is a common age for great frustration stemming from the child's own perceived limitations rather than from parental opposition or restriction. This is confusing to parents, and they become frustrated themselves with children this age.

When children between age four and six have tantrums, the parents' goal should be to help teach the child how to express frustration appropriately rather than to alleviate the frustration. At this

age most children cannot relieve their frustration by words alone; th
need a physical outlet as well.

Again, at the end of the temper tantrum, discussing the cause of t
frustration, reassuring the child that everyone gets frustrated, and be
physically close to the child promotes bonding. The parents' modelli
the way they themselves cope with frustration is very important. Th
parent who abuses his child or others when he is frustrated has not y
learned to handle his own frustration appropriately and is poorly
equipped to help the child handle his feelings.

Hopefully, by the time the child reaches early adolescence, he wi
have learned the appropriate ways to express his frustration, since th
is normally a time of increased frustration and impulsivity. Because (
aggressive impulses and their increased physical size adolescents
themselves are fearful of their own reaction to anger and frustration
and they may seek to be alone — even by running away — as an atten
to deal with these feelings in a non-harmful way.

## Conscience development and values incorporation

What is conscience? According to Selma Fraiberg (1959), 'Conscienc
consists of a set of standards and prohibitions which have been taken
over by the personality and which govern behaviour from within'.

Attachment is related to conscience development. The child must
fear the loss of the love of someone he is attached to and trusts if he
is to develop a conscience. This does not mean that adults need to
threaten the child with loss of love. The fear is already there; it is
overwhelming to the child to be threatened directly. Threats of
abandonment or loss of love undermine the child's sense of trust for
the adult.

The greatest inherent fear of a three-year-old child is that his moth
may abandon him. If this occurs repeatedly, the child does not learn
trust and to feel secure in the presence of others. There is no
foundation for conscience development.

Conscience development takes a number of years to be completed;
it doesn't occur in a matter of days, weeks, or months. Most children
are nine or ten before their conscience is ingrained enough so that the
feel guilty when they are quite sure they won't be caught. Until that
stage, children feel best if they are receiving adequate supervision fror
adults so they don't have to struggle to maintain self control that is
beyond their abilities. Conscience development continues throughout
the primary and secondary years and is not complete until the
adolescent is completely independent of his parents. Values continue
to change during adult years as well.

Unfortunately, the word 'guilt' has received a bad reputation in the
past few years. Much is said and written about the dangers of too muc
guilt, but guilt needs to be kept in balance. Too much guilt is
paralysing; however, too little guilt is dangerous. Adolescents and
adults with no conscience may steal, assault, and murder without guilt

## Conscience development in toddlers

As a toddler, the child only experiences guilt when he receives or anticipates disapproval from the outside. He stops himself from touching a desirable object only when he knows that it will incur his parents' disapproval and/or discipline. It is very important that parents give very clear messages about which behaviour they approve and which they disapprove. These do not need to be lengthy explanations; in fact, such explanations may be detrimental in the long run. Initially the disapproval can be expressed by the word 'no' said in a no-nonsense tone.

Approval can be conveyed by the single word 'good' spoken in a soft, approving tone and accompanied by a caress. When the child is speaking in short sentences around age three, short sentences can be used to express the approval or disapproval; for example, 'I really like it when you do this,' or 'I don't like that behaviour at all.' As the child approaches school age, simple explanations of the reasons for disapproving of his behaviour should be given. Messages starting with the word 'I' are more helpful than those starting with 'you'. 'You' messages too often become a form of name calling.

## Conscience development in pre-school children

Four and five year olds are at one and the same time the most truthful and untruthful of creatures. Basically they are very honest, often to the embarrassment of their parents, because they lack 'tact'. At the same time, they certainly are not above projecting blame onto another, even an imaginary friend at a pinch. Adults generally demand that their children always tell the truth. However, frequently this is not what they truly want the children to do.

*'I remember being in a lift with my four-and-a-half year old daughter and a man who was a stranger to us. My daughter carefully scrutinised him and then offered, "You know, you would look better without a beard." Although she was merely expressing her honest opinion, I certainly was embarrassed!'*

Frequently when children say something bluntly truthful, either about an adult or another child, parents reply, 'You don't really mean that.' This is especially common when the four or five-year-old honestly expresses his feelings about a sibling with 'I hate him.' Parents consistently try to talk the child out of being honest. The brutally honest way that children of this age express strong feelings seems to make adults feel very uncomfortable. Adults seem to forget the transitory nature of feelings.

Parents must reassess their own values when they are dealing with pre-school-age children. Frequently parents hold two values that are at times incompatible. Take for example 'honesty' and 'respect for your elders.' When these two values conflict, which value is the child to choose? Parents need to clarify and even rank their own values if it is important to them to transmit them to their child.

Usually we want a child to be honest about his own behaviour; hopefully, we can accept his honesty about his own strong feelings.

When it comes to comments about others, we want them to be honest as long as they have something positive to say, but otherwise to keep quiet! This the child learns as he acquires a sense of tact.

The years between four and six are crucial for conscience development. Most children do a number of things that their parents don't like during this period. Most of the time they are under the supervision of their parents or another adult, which is an important requirement for conscience development.

It is rarely necessary and usually dangerous to begin an exchange with a pre-school child with a phrase like 'Who took the cookies?' or whatever. At this age it is common to see the trail of cookie crumbs leading directly to the culprit who still has the remains around his mouth. If the parent asks 'Who took the cookies?' she is sure to get 'Not me' in response despite the evidence to the contrary. If the parent moves to 'Don't lie to me; I know you did it,' then the child feels deceived since the parent implied message in 'Who took the cookies?' is that the parent doesn't already know the answer.

The parent who understands conscience development and wants to aid in its development says 'I see you took the cookies; you know that I don't like that. Now you just sit down here until you can tell me about it.' The implied message in this is 'I already know what is going on so there is no advantage to lying; in fact the advantage is in telling the truth.'

If the parents are trying to encourage honesty about misbehaviour, then they should not punish the child after he tells the truth. The implied message in this is 'You get into trouble telling the truth; learn to be a better liar.' If the rule infraction is one that needs more direct discipline then it's not the time to work on honesty, but 'I know that you did so and so, and this is what is going to happen because of it.'

The most useful adjuncts to the development of conscience at this age are parents' 'Big eyes and ears' that keep track of the child's activities. That is why children commonly think parents have eyes in the back of their heads — a useful misperception in terms of conscience development. Mother's big eyes and ears should not be limited to use in negative situations. She can make positive comments like 'It certainly sounded as though you were having fun playing in your room.' The important thing is for the child to feel that his parent already knows what is going on with him and that he might as well be truthful.

Since this is such a necessary stage of normal conscience development, it becomes apparent why it is difficult to aid conscience development when it is delayed and children are old enough to be out of parents' supervision much of the time.

The next step is noticing when the child stops himself from misbehaving and positively reinforcing this. An example will serve to clarify this.

### Case example

*I was seeing an eight-year-old in counselling with his parents. He had been moved several times before being placed in his adoptive home at age 7 and did not have much trust in adults. Understandably, he had delayed conscience development.*

*His dishonesty was of great concern to his parents. Much of the counselling was aimed at helping the parents help the child develop a conscience. One day when the mother happened to glance out of the upstairs window, she saw the boy start to do something he had repeatedly been reprimanded about, then glance up at the window, and stop himself. Though she was beyond his sight, just the thought that she might be there enabled him to stop himself. Later his mother commented 'I noticed you stopped yourself from doing so and so today; that's really good.' This told the child two things; first, 'I still know what is going on, and I would have stopped you if you hadn't stopped yourself' and second, 'I like it when you can control yourself, and I don't have to.'*

### Conscience development in older children

By the time the child is six, parents can usually learn to tell the special way that each child has of expressing his anxiety when he is being untruthful. For one it is avoiding eye contact; for another it may be frequent licking of the lips, gulping or rapid clenching and releasing of the fists. Once the parents have learned to identify these 'give-aways' with certainty they should share their knowledge with the child. For example they should say 'Your mouth is telling me one thing, but your eyes are telling me something else. I have learned to believe your eyes in this situation.'

Many parents are reluctant to do this. However, a 'guilty' conscience occurs when the child feels uncomfortable internally when he does something 'wrong' even when he does not fear being caught and punished by another. This internalised guilty feeling is usually associated with a feeling of anxiety. Helping the child to recognise these feelings and his own behaviour demonstrates to him that he is capable of telling the truth himself. The parent can say to the child 'Pay attention to your eyes; what are they saying?' This method starts to hook the eyes and the mouth up to give a congruent message. It also helps the child to recognise his own discomfort and correct his own behaviour.

It is usually during these years between six and ten that the child begins to confront his parents about discrepancies between their actions and words. At this stage of development the child might ask 'How come you say "always be honest", but you told me to tell the salesman you weren't home?'

In the past children were not exposed to as many different value systems as they now confront. Communities and neighbourhoods were more homogeneous. The child's friends, neighbours, teachers and schoolmates were more likely to hold values not too different from those he learned at home.

In more recent years communities and neighbourhoods are comprised of families with varying values. The child, even in his early school years, may be exposed to values in sharp contrast to those held by the parents. In addition the influence of television in terms of value judgments is considerable.

Wise parents will make sure that their children have contact with other families who have similar values. This becomes very important during the adolescent years. At this time the young person is more open to learning values outside the home than in the home environment. It is usual for an adolescent to use an adult other than his own parent to confide in. This confidant may be the parent of a friend or it may be a young adult. Parents should try to ensure that their adolescent has opportunities to confide in other adults who hold values similar to their own.

It is not uncommon for an adolescent to come home with 'news' that so and so believes such and such. Frequently this is the same value that the parents think they have been stressing themselves. However, it is best if they take an approach of interest and acceptance, rather than exclaiming 'What do you think I've been trying to teach you!'

With the older child parents should teach values at times when the child is not under pressure. When the child does not feel that a message is aimed at changing him, he is more likely to hear it and accept it. The larger part of value teaching takes place prior to adolescence. Yet many parents think that they can wait until those crucial years and then make their impact. Age ten is an ideal time for value teaching. Children at ten are old enough to understand, yet young enough to accept parental values more readily.

Adolescents frequently go through a period in which they reject their parents' values. Some of this seems to be necessary for them to separate from the family. The parents must manage to assert that their values have worked well for them without getting into control battles over them. Parents who achieve this are quite likely to find that the adolescent chooses to accept most of his parents' values as he becomes an adult. This acceptance comes because the adolescent chooses the values rather than bending to pressure.

Unfortunately many parents try to make control issues of values. This is rarely successful. The statement 'You may not ever smoke pot' is impossible to enforce unless the parent keeps the adolescent under his eye all of the time. 'You may not smoke pot in our house' is certainly easier to enforce. If parents make clear statements about what they approve or disapprove of, it is not the same as making a control issue out of a particular value. Again, they should take care to start their declarations with 'I think ..........' or 'I believe ........' rather than 'You may not ..........'.

Exercise 7 that follows gives you an opportunity to consider conscience development issues that face the adoptive parents of a youngster in placement.

*Exercise 7:*
Working with delayed conscience development

Instructions

*Purpose:*

To help you learn about children with delayed conscience development and think about strategies for working with them.

*How to do it:*

1. Read Sharon's case history. (See also *Attachment and separation BAAF 1981*)

2. Answer the questions on the worksheet for Exercise 7. Then compare your own answers with those of another caseworker on the sample worksheet.

## Sharon's Case

Sharon is an eight-year-old girl who is being placed for adoption in a family with three older boys. Past history reveals that Sharon experienced considerable emotional and physical deprivation, rejection, and physical abuse from her birth parents. She has had seve moves since she first came into care at age three.

Sharon has many fears including fear of the dark and fear of new situations. She is prone to nightmares. There is a history of both day-time and night-time wetting. She is a very demanding child who verbally pressures and manipulates adults. She gets little pleasure from being a child and prefers to 'pretend' that she is an adolescent going o on dates. She is very seductive in her relationship with males.

Sharon has many gaps in her basic fund of knowledge; she exhibits problems with logical thinking and basis cause and effect. Sharon has many problems with lying; she tends to 'forget' what she chooses not to hear. Her lying extends even to saying 'that is my favourite food' when in reality it is a food she dislikes. At other times her lying is aimed at keeping out of trouble.

She has marked difficulties with peer relationships. She does well i the self-help skills. She likes to help with household tasks. In school, she is reading above her age level but has some difficulty with maths. She shows appropriate affect and is an attractive girl who is quite outgoing. Her self-esteem is poor as indicated by comments such as 'something is wrong with me', when she makes an error. She is able to talk about feelings and can tell of many ways that she and her present foster parents have fun together.

Sharon picks up money from around the house and denies it. Frequently she comes home from school with pencils, small amounts of money, and other small objects that she claims to have 'found'. She sometimes lies about unimportant, inconsequential things that she would not be punished for doing. It has been noted that when she lies, Sharon's eyes become very large and her gaze is very direct. She frequently says 'and that's the truth' at this time. Sharon's adoptive mother teaches at the school that Sharon attends.

*Exercise 7:*
**Working with delayed conscience development**

Worksheet

1. At what age level does Sharon seem to be functioning in terms of conscience development?

2. What specific advice would you give to the adoptive parents about dealing with Sharon's various types of lying?

3. What would be your advice about the 'found' objects?

4. You may also choose to give suggestions about her fears and her preference to 'pretend' that she is an adolescent.

*Exercise 7:*
## Working with delayed conscience development

### Sample Worksheet

1. At what age level does Sharon seem to be functioning in terms of conscience development?

   She is functioning at a 'pre-school' level in terms of conscious development.

2. What specific advice would you give to the adoptive parents about dealing with Sharon's various types of lying?

   Make it clear that they know when she is lying — her eyes give her away. Encourage honesty about misbehaviour. Keep track of her activities so that she feels the parents know what is going on and she might as well be truthful and praise her.

3. What would be your advice about the 'found' objects?

   Check with the school and return anything that had not been 'found'.

4. You may also choose to give suggestions about her fears and her preference to 'pretend' that she is an adolescent.

   Help the parents recognise these as the fears and behaviour of a younger child. Develop bed time rituals and encourage attachment behaviour. Give her more sex education, help her to become attached to mother and identify with her. Let her see that she can gain father's affection and approval without being sexually provocative.

## Sexual development

From a very early age the child's pleasurable sexual feelings are inhibited by parents. For instance, the mouth which is a source of pleasure to babies, becomes 'off limits' for anything except food. Even fingers and thumbs are frequently prohibited.

The child learns early on that there are certain other parts of the body, which to them seem associated with elimination, that they are not to touch. The confusing thing for the child is that these are precisely the areas of the body that are the most pleasant to touch. Gradually, most pre-school children learn that while they cannot touch their sexual organs in public, they may do it in private. However, they are likely to feel guilty if they do so. At the same time they learn that although they may touch many parts of their parents' bodies, other parts are 'off limits'.

By age two and a half the child's sense of identity is strongly associated with his sex and position in the family. For each family there are different expectations for the oldest girl, oldest boy, youngest child, and so on. The family's expectations and the degree to which the child achieves them become part of the child's sense of himself and affect his self esteem.

The young child gets good feelings about himself if he perceives that his sexuality is valued by both parents. If either parent does not value the child's sexuality, then the child is likely to develop problems with self esteem and have difficulty feeling comfortable with his own sexual identity.

The Oedipal stage occurs between the ages of four and six and is characterised by the child competing with the parent of the same sex for the attention of the parent of the opposite sex.

As a result of the child's tendency for magical thinking at this age, if he has occasional fantasies about harm coming to the parent of the same sex, he is likely to be afraid these fantasies will come true. The child may act out in the presence of the parent of the same sex so that the parent will get angry and punish him. This alleviates some of his guilt for his 'bad' thoughts.

It is best if the parent of the same sex as the child takes an active part in handling any overt demonstrations of the Oedipal conflict in the child. The parent can reassure the child that he had these same feelings when he was a child; that they are normal; and that the parents understand these feelings and are not upset by them.

The usual mode of resolution of the Oedipal concerns is through identification with the parent of the same sex. The child of the latency age years tends to have friends of the same sex. Boys tend to want to do chores with dad and help him work in the yard or on the car, while girls stay in and help mother with the housework.

Youngsters at the Oedipal stage become aware of the fact that their parents have a 'private' life that occurs in their bedroom and is not shared with the child. The child's natural curiosity about sex should be satisfied by talking or reading books with the parents rather than by observing the parents undressed or engaged in sexual intercourse.

Young latency age children enjoy the book 'Where did I come from?' (Mayle, 1973); however, many parents do not like the pictures in this book or its explicit nature. This book is included in a list of publications on sex education recommended by the National Marriage Guidance Council. The Family Planning Association and Health Education Council also provide lists of recommended leaflets, many available free of charge.

As children enter adolescence, they may become aroused by demonstrations of affection from the parent of the opposite sex. The child may become very uncomfortable about such expressions of affection and think themselves 'weird' to be sexually aroused by their parents. The adolescent can usually accept spontaneous physical expressions of affection such as a quick hug or kiss on the cheek. Physical horseplay also sometimes leads to strong sexual feelings in the adolescent. Thus, it should be avoided between parents and children of the opposite sex or between siblings of the opposite sex.

It is helpful to adolescents if there have always been commonsense rules about privacy and some measure of modesty around the house. This protects the adolescent from feeling sexually aroused by parental or sibling figures. Most adolescents feel guilty if they are sexually aroused by a parent or sibling and yet during early adolescence sexual arousal can occur with quite minimal stimulation. Parents need to respect the privacy of their children as much as they expect the children to respect their privacy.

The adolescent uses the parent of the same sex as a sex role model; he chooses to be like the parent of the same sex in some ways and chooses to be different in others. At the same time, the young adolescent uses the parent, or other parents, of the opposite sex to win both confirmation and approval for his own emerging sexuality. The older adolescent seeks confirmation and approval of his sexuality from his peers.

Young people entering their teens want and need sex education. 'So now you know about sex' is a Family Doctor book which offers a straightforward and factual account of sexual terms and techniques for 13-year-olds and upwards.

Exercise 8 which follows gives an example of the problems seen in the sexually abused adolescent. You will have an opportunity to outline a plan for meeting the adolescent's developmental needs.

*Exercise 8:*
Identifying the developmental needs in a sexually abused adolescent

Instructions

*Purpose:*

To give you an opportunity to identify developmental needs in the adolescent who has been sexually abused and to develop a plan to meet those needs.

*How to do it:*

1. Read Debbie's case history.

2. Answer the questions on the worksheet for Exercise 8. Then, compare your own answers with those of another caseworker on the sample worksheet.

### Debbie's case

*Debbie is 14. Her mother physically abused her, and her step-father started sexually abusing her when she was 11. Debbie reported the abuse to a school counsellor. When the police became involved because of the sexual abuse, Debbie's mother and step-father left the area, leaving Debbie with a neighbour.*

*Subsequently, the mother's parental rights were terminated. Debbie's birth father, who lives in another area, was contacted about having Debbie to live with him. He expressed some interest but didn't follow through. So his parental rights were also terminated.*

*Debbie has had three foster placements since she was 11 and a half All of her foster parents have described her as a sexually provocative child. She is seen as wilful and disobedient with foster mothers, although she usually obeys the foster fathers. She is also viewed as a manipulator.*

*During the past two years her grades have dropped from primarily As and Bs to primarily Cs and Ds. She has peer problems; most of her friends are boys and girls who also have many problems. Most of them have been in trouble with the law.*

*Debbie says repeatedly that everything would be fine if she could live with her dad whom she hasn't seen for five years. She blames the judge and social workers for keeping them apart. She phones her father, and he always accepts her reverse charge calls. She tends to see her birth father as 'super', while she sees her birth mother as 'a rotten no good whore'.*

*Recently she ran away from her foster home after being punished for not coming home on time. The foster family has requested that she be moved.*

*A maternal aunt who lives about 100 miles away has expressed an interest in Debbie. There is also a local family who have expressed an interest in adopting an adolescent like Debbie.*

*Exercise 8:*

**Identifying the developmental needs in a sexually abused adolescent**

Worksheet

1. What are the indications of separation — individuation problems? Develop a plan for helping to resolve these problems.

2. What are the indications of control issue problems? What advice would you give to parental figures about handling these issues.

3. What are the indications of problems in the sexual areas? Outline a plan for meeting Debbie's developmental needs in this area.

**Identifying the developmental needs in a sexually abused adolescent**

## Sample Worksheet

1. What are the indications of separation — individuation problems?
   Develop a plan for helping to resolve these problems.

   Debbie opposes foster family rules, values and expectations. She
   cannot come to a resolution about the separation and loss of her
   parents and seeing mother as all bad and father as all good.
   She should not be protected from father's rejection — this
   should be brought out into the open. Her anger with the social
   worker should be verbalised. She needs more information about
   her own mother and help to understand her problems.

2. What are the indications of control issue problems? What advice would
   you give to parental figures about handling these issues.

   Involve Debbie in discussions about moves and other issues.
   Get verbal or written commitments about what she will work at
   to make a placement succeed. This can be referred back to in
   a conflict and will help her to take responsibility for her own
   behaviour.

3. What are the indications of problems in the sexual areas? Outline a plan
   for meeting Debbie's developmental needs in this area.

   She is sexually provocative, she obeys her foster father's
   and is wilful and disobedient with foster mothers. She needs
   some good sex education and she needs some affectionate
   and non-sexual relationships with adults, particularly
   a woman with whom she can identify.

# Sources

Ainsworth, M.D. and Boston, M., 'Psychodiagnostic assessments of a child after prolonged separation in early childhood', *Brit. Journal Med. Psychol.*, 25: 169 − 201, 1952.

Committee on Adolescence, *Normal adolescence: its dynamics and impact*, Group for Advancement of Psychiatry, New York, 1968, Vol VI, Report 68, 1968.

Elmer, E., and Gregg, G., 'Developmental characteristics of abused children', *Pediatrics*, 40 (4): 596 − 602, 1967.

Fahlberg, V., *Attachment and separation*, *BAAF*, 1981 and *Helping children when they must move*, *BAAF*, 1982.

Fraiburg, S., *The magic years*, Charles Scribner and Son, New York/Methuen, 1959.

Gesell, A., *et al*, *The first five years of life: the pre-school years*, Harper and Row, New York, 1940.

Gesell, A., and Ilg, F., *The child from five to ten*, Harper and Row, New York, 1946.

Hymes, J.L., *The child under six*, Prentice Hall, New Jersey, 1969.

Jewett, C., 'Adolescent adjustments', lecture given in Lakewood, Colorado, 1980.

Mayle, P., *Where did I come from?*, Lyle Stewart, New Jersey/Macmillan, 1973.

Wolff, P.H., *The causes, controls and organization of behavior in the neonate*, International Universities Press, New York, 1966.

Lists of sex education pamphlets and leaflets may be obtained from:

Family Planning Association
27 Mortimer Street
London W1

National Marriage Guidance Council
Herbert Gray College
Little Church Street
Rugby CV21 3AP

Printed by
Witley Press Ltd, Norfolk

Designed by
Ivor Kamlish FSIAD & Associates